This work is written in praise of my Lord and Savior Jesus Christ. Thank you Jesus for my *wife*, my *son*, my *life*.

— CONTENTS —

Foreword

Foreword
by Dr. Mark Cress, Founder
Corporate Chaplains of America

As long as there have been businesses in the United States, there have been Christian business owners hoping to please God through the efforts of their work. Since the early 1990s, a movement has blossomed, giving way to a new type of Christian free- enterprise leader who is desirous of building his business—to the glory of God—as a platform for ministry. Thousands of such leaders are cropping up in all corners of the United States. As of 2011, it has been estimated that non-profit organizations that cater to this movement have grown from as few as fifty members at their inception to over 2,000 members. Scores of books have been written about various aspects of how God is at "work" in the workplace.

Consider, the real heavy cream always rises to the top and this is where guys like Peter Freissle come into the picture. When we first met Peter, it was clear that God had touched his heart regarding the workplace ministry movement, as well as deepening his affection for people, especially, his employees. Peter's company manufactures screen media for the mining industry, and one day one of his clients—a fellow by the name of Darryl Lanker—shared a business card with him. By the time of their encounter, Darryl had been active in the workplace ministry movement for over a decade and his commitment to Jesus Christ was clearly displayed on the back of his business card. This simple exchange of business cards had a profound impact on Peter's life and he felt empowered to dive even deeper into the movement.

Time passed and Peter had long since printed the core values of his company on the reverse of his company's business cards which espoused his Christian virtues and desire to honor God in everything. In fact, I have heard several stories of how God has worked in the lives of various people, as a direct result of the message located on the back of those business cards. Since that time, Peter has become a leader among other Christian business owners in the movement. Peter and Scott Gajewsky—a fellow who has become a dear friend to me—even formed a non-profit ministry called His Way At Work, to help spread the word regarding many aspects of the workplace ministry movement.

One day Peter, Scott and I were having lunch with another long term leader in the workplace ministry movement, my close friend Dr. Steve Steff. Steve was working on a leadership book at the time and was interviewing Peter for a section in that book. Steve, a gifted communicator, was fascinated by the stories I had been sharing with him about how God was at work at Peter's company, Polydeck. At one point during our lunch, while I was in a conversation with Scott, Peter spoke with Steve. As Peter shared one story after another about how God had blessed the language on the back of his business card, Scott and I stopped and just listened. It was abundantly clear to all of us that God was at work in this conversation. Finally, with a strong sense of God's leading, I suggested that Steve and Scott work closely with Peter to produce a book about the business card. After lunch, as soon as we returned to Polydeck, we went straight to the chapel located in the business and prayed for God's guidance about such a book project. By Monday of the following week, Steve had agreed to take the lead in writing the book; likewise, Scott offered his assistance in providing details and handling the logistics of the project. The leadership team at Lanphier Press quickly embraced the project and we were off to the races.

Whether currently in the workplace ministry movement or considering taking the leap, our prayer is that God will use this little book to encourage thousands of business leaders. On behalf of Peter, Steve, Scott, the entire Lanphier Press team, and myself…we wish you God's very best and pray you will be blessed for taking time to read *The Business Card*.

Part 1
—Chapter 1—

Be Careful
How You Pray

One evening Peter drove through the streets of Johannesburg with his father. While it was a beautiful evening, Peter was distracted by his thoughts—he had been troubled in discerning God's will and direction for his family, as well as the family business. For most of his adult life, Peter had been groomed for the role of CEO in the multi-national business that his father and his father's friend had started in 1958. Peter understood that such a commitment would have to be thought through prayerfully and carefully. The two men were deep in conversation, when suddenly an old car crossed their path and broke down right in front of them. Even more odd, two men jumped out from the car carrying brooms that were covered with trash bags. What could possibly be going on?

In disbelief, Peter and his father gazed at the scene unfolding before their eyes—the brooms and trash bags erupted in flashes of light and deafening noise. The brooms were in fact, AK-47 assault rifles, and they were spraying bullets directly at the car where Peter and his father were sitting. The noise was deafening, and shards of glass were flying all around them. Armor-piercing bullets riddled the car as both attackers emptied the magazines of their weapons. While attempting to flee the scene Peter came to his senses just long enough to steer the car around their attackers. Both Peter and his father were covered in blood, but with adrenaline pumping through their veins, neither of the men knew the nature of their injuries. There was no time for fear or panic. Peter knew of a hospital only a few blocks away and headed toward it as fast as he could drive.

Upon arriving at the hospital and being examined thoroughly by the doctors, neither Peter nor his father had been hit by the rain of bullets; however, both of them had been peppered by the exploding glass. This was truly a miracle that the two men were still alive. How could their attackers have emptied their weapons into Peter's vehicle, only a few feet from them and not hit either Peter or his father?

Toward the end of Peter's examination, a nurse commented on the strange hole in his shirt. As they looked more closely, the evidence was clear. Apparently, a bullet had entered through the left side of Peter's shirt and traveled between the shirt and his chest, and exited through the sleeve of his right arm. This armor-piercing bullet had traveled a fraction of an inch across his entire body.

Is it possible to experience such an attack, have

evidence of bullets passing through your clothing, and walk away virtually unharmed? While many would call the experience a mere coincidence or act of fate, but to Peter it was clear as day—this was no *co-incidence*, but rather a *God-incidence*. Peter left the hospital that day with only two thoughts: "Thank you, Lord, for sparing my life." "Thank you, Lord, for answering my prayer."

Prior to the attack that evening, Peter had been praying about whether to relocate his family to the United States or remain in South Africa, but he had sensed no clear direction on the matter. Within a month after the attack Peter and his family were in Spartanburg, South Carolina. As Peter reflects back on that terrible night, he shares that now when he prays for God's will, he waits and listens for that "still small voice."

Reflection

How many times have you told a friend, "I'll pray for you," or "We'll be praying for you," only to move on to the next on your agenda and never give the issues a second thought? Far too often Christians seem to pray out of obligation or habit. Consider, are you praying because it is your turn to pray at the meeting? Are you praying because you are getting ready to eat—everyone knows that you are supposed to pray before you eat, right? Out of habit, are you praying because it is the last thing you do at night before going to sleep? Maybe you pray just before you get on an airplane.

Prayer is supposed to be a form of communication, as well as a conversation with the living God. Imagine, a friend that you have dedicated your life to care for, protecting, and providing their every need. In addition, you have wept over the pain that they have felt and the mistakes they have made. You may have bailed them out of one mess after another; yet every time you get together to visit with your friend they say the same over and over, never listening to you or asking what you think; thus never really carrying on a conversation. It is as if they are just "checking in," like an obligation. Sooner or later, you would recognize this as a one-way relationship. They are not coming to you because

18

they love you or care to be with you; likewise, they are not coming to you out of respect or seeking advice. To this end, they are there out of habit, or because they are afraid you might cut them off as a "friend."

In Luke 11:5–10, there is what is often referred to as the *Parable of the Persistent Friend*. Jesus told the story of a man who had a house guest, and had nothing to feed the guest. Late in the night the "seeking" man went to the house of another friend, knocked on his door, and "pleads his need" through the closed door. He was not met with a very welcome response. The home-owner was in bed, his children were in bed, and it was midnight. "Go away!" But the "seeking" man persisted. He couldn't give up. His need was too great and there was only one man that he could count on.

The Scripture goes on to explain that the home-owner was not going to get rousted out of bed because he was a friend, but eventually he would respond due to the persistence of the "seeking" man. "And I say to you, ask, and it shall be given to you; seek, and you shall find; knock, and the door shall be opened to you. For everyone who asks, receives; and he who seeks, finds; and to him who knocks, it shall be opened." (Luke 5:9–10)

Another well-known verse is located in Philippians 4:6, "Be anxious for nothing, but in every-thing by prayer and supplication with thanksgiving let your requests be made known to God." If we are to have a true relationship with God, then we must commit time to that relationship. God has broad shoulders. Share everything with Him and allow time for Him to respond, and trust that His wisdom will guide you in the path that is His absolute best for you. Be persistent. Pray, and pray again for He will answer. He always does.

— CHAPTER 2—

GOD IS
A SLICE

Following his life-changing experience, there was no question in Peter Freissle's mind that it was time to leave South Africa. In 1994, Peter moved his family to Spartanburg, SC, where his Dad, Manfred Freissle and Dieter Egler—his business partner—had started a business in 1978—Polydeck. God blessed Peter with a wonderful family and a great opportunity to grow the business in the United States. When Peter relocated to South Carolina, the company only had 30 employees. Yet by 2005, sales had grown rapidly, employing well over 100 individuals in the surrounding area, as well as a sales team scattered around the globe. It did not seem as if life could be better.

Peter had grown up in the business and felt blessed to have had a loving Dad that taught him the "ropes" of the business from a young age. From his Dad's example, Peter knew that to be successful in business he must work hard, work smart, and be fully committed to the business. And committed he was, for like many hard-driven businessmen, Peter spent so many hours at the office that his wife often commented that he might as well sleep there. That way he would not be wasting all his time driving back-and-forth.

In addition, having grown up in the church, Peter knew that ultimately, somehow, God was in control of everything, and Peter was faithful to thank God when he worshipped with his family. Work hard, live a good life, you do your part, and God will do His. These were the principles by which Peter lived his life. After almost ten years of living in the United States, the intense focus on the business had diluted the connection that Peter had experienced with God the day of the shooting. To this end, God seemed distant in some way.

In the summer of 2005, it was clear that Polydeck was headed for another banner year. Sales continued to climb, the economy was strong, and Peter had put together a team that knew how to get the job done. The only problem with the whole picture was that Peter was tired. Hard-charging all the time, and being the father of four children under the age of ten, does not leave much time for rest or relaxation.

It was at this point that a friend of Peter's invited him to Atlanta for a "silent retreat" that is known as "Spiritual Exercises of Ignatius of Loyola." Peter did not exactly understand what a "silent retreat" was, but the idea of a few days of silence was inviting. More important than that, Peter knew that there was a persistent emptiness in him that he just could not shake. Yes, he was living the "American

Dream," business was doing well, and his family was good—everyone was healthy. Yet, there was still something missing in Peter's life. He was to the point that he was willing to do whatever was necessary to figure out what was missing in his life.

The trip to Atlanta was great, but the problem was that the retreat was anything but silent. Peter's first revelation on the retreat was: if you run fast enough and work hard enough, you will not hear your wife, you probably will not hear your co-workers, and you certainly will not hear God. Forced as it was, the "silence" together with the inspirational talks given by the retreat pastor, allowed Peter to hear God speak as he had never heard Him before.

Peter was quite familiar with biblical principles, and he understood the concept of making God a part of his life, but he had never sat down and determined exactly what that meant. "God is a part of my life, but what part?" Peter knew that God wanted him to analyze his life and to look honestly at what his life consisted of—was he the same on the inside as what he professed to be on the outside?

During his professional life, Peter had taken part in hundreds of presentations; he grabbed a large piece of paper and started to draw, just as if he were presenting to his company board of directors. He started with a large circle and divided it into the important areas of his life. The process was painful, because as Peter became more honest with himself, one segment of the circle continued to grow. With the segment continuing to grow, the remaining segments were getting smaller and smaller. The large segment had a simple title, ME. Peter began to realize that all of his time, energy, and resources were dedicated to ME. In his professional life, Peter worked hard to be successful; thus, ME would receive various forms of glory and praise. Peter worked hard to provide for his family so the ME could be recognized as the best father and provider for his family.

OLD COMPARTMENTALIZED ME

From the diagram, Peter realized that he did not

need this recognition from friends and family, but he needed it for the ME inside himself. A distant second to the ME was Peter's wife and family. He loved them with all his heart, at least all of his heart to which he had access. While Peter affectionately remembered reflecting on the unconditional love his mother had showered him with as a child and the loving home environment she had created for him, he had lost this unconditional love for his family.

Sadly, in third place behind ME and his family, was God. If you had met Peter the week before and asked him about his relationship with God, he would have told you that he had a great relationship with God and that he and his family attended church regularly. On that day he realized that it was all a lie. Peter was religious, but not in love with God. Suddenly, Peter looked at the circle and realized that the God he had read about, talked about, and heard about all of his life, was nothing more in his life than a slice on a diagram, and a very small slice at that. While gazing at the diagram, it was undeniable; Peter realized that this was not a mere epiphany. God did not simply speak to Peter; God had broken Peter to a point of repentance.

Looking at the drawing, Peter realized that much of his life was plainly wrong. God continued to speak to Peter and to remove the blinders from his eyes. Peter started to become aware that the life he had worked so hard at, where he had achieved so much worldly success, was worth no Eternal value. Peter realized that day that everything that he had and everything that he had accomplished in business, had been given to him by God for one simple purpose, to draw Peter closer to God through Jesus Christ, the Master of the Universe. The *Parable of the Talents* kept ringing in his head, and he realized, God would not be asking me "How much money did you make" but would ask, "What did you do with the money I gave you? Did you use it to glorify and please yourself, or to glorify Me?"

Realization and Redemption

Consider, if you came to the realization that everything that you thought you had accomplished in your life was done through you and not by you, because of the gifts given to you. Also, consider that you forged ahead in life with hardly a "thank you" or acknowledgement to those that had supported you; likewise, you did not use the gifts of time, money, and authority, to please God, but employed them selfishly or even used them to hurt or manipulate other people. Once you realized how you had been living your life, what possible response could there be but, FORGIVE ME.

Finally, the story of forgiveness that Peter had heard all of his life meant something. It was a story that he had always known, that God gave His Son that we might be forgiven. Yet, it was a story that held little value in Peter's day-to-day life. Knowing his past and even his present, Peter felt unworthy of forgiveness. After a time of reflection, he realized that it was this feeling of unworthiness that had allowed him, even required him, to keep his business life separate from his personal life. It was only after God had revealed the true meaning behind success and accomplishment that Peter realized he needed forgiveness for every day of his life. Forgiveness for every thought that failed to give God the glory. Forgiveness for a lack of gratitude and respect for his employees and for treating them as mere inputs of production rather than the neighbors God had called him to love. In addition, Peter was called to forgiveness for failing to realize that even the love that he received so abundantly from his wife and children was a gift from God. The realization of the depths of his selfishness and pride—sin—overwhelmed him.

Such a realization, such pain and grief, could only come from God; thus conviction. Certainly, there was no human reasoning that Peter would put himself through this agony. Possessing insight such as this was no mere coincidence, rather a miracle hand-delivered by the Holy Spirit; however, the real miracle was yet to come. Peter's background in church had not only taught him about sin and the need for forgiveness, it had taught him how this forgiveness was accomplished. Peter knew that forgiveness was as simple as asking Jesus Christ to forgive him for a life of sin, but of such magnitude that Jesus died on the cross for our sins, and through his blood we find forgiveness. Based on the atoning work of Jesus, Peter knew that his sins had been forgiven. Amazing! A miracle! Yes, a divine miracle.

Peter described the moment as literally feeling that he had been washed all over, completely. Not just washed on the outside as to remove the dirt of the world, but as if his soul had been scrubbed clean. It was clear, the Peter that traveled to Atlanta to get away from work for a few days, and discover the source of the emptiness, would not be the same Peter that returned to South Carolina.

God could no longer be a simple slice of Peter's life. Peter longed for God to be the center of his life, and that God's will and love should permeate and affect all the decisions in every area his life. Then, he realized that as long as God would remain in the center of his life, it would give meaning and purpose—eternal purpose—and fill the emptiness that the world and its treasures could *not* fill.

Peter knew that if he was going to become the man that God desired him to be, it would require a painful examination of who he was, not to mention gut-wrenching honesty. Peter knew that he had completely altered the way he thought and his approach to life; likewise, he knew that one of the most difficult alterations must occur in how he approached his business.

During the drive back to Spartanburg, Peter reflected on this new relationship with Jesus and the impact that it would have on his relationships, most importantly, his wife and family. Suddenly it came to him, all of those times in the past when Peter had been inconsiderate and even unkind to his wife, and her reaction was to "graciously forgive him." In response to the aforementioned event, Peter would often bring his wife flowers on the following day. As he continued to think through such events, it occurred to Peter that he didn't bring flowers so that his wife would forgive him. He brought flowers BE-CAUSE she had forgiven him. That was it! That was what he had been missing out on all this time. That was what he had never understood.

In this same way, Peter has understood that any service he might give to Jesus was not an offering so that he might be forgiven, it was a response *because he had been forgiven*. It was this burning feeling of gratitude that began the search for ways to show God how *grateful* he was for the incredible gift of forgiveness and unconditional love. This was the greatest gift Peter had ever received. As Peter left Atlanta, he felt like a fire was burning within him.

NEW GOD CENTERED ME

Now, Peter had a burning desire to accomplish two things. First, he had a desire to reconcile the wrongs he had done to so many people—his wife, family, friends, and employees. Second, Peter had a burning desire to share his incredible experience of God's unconditional *love* with as many people as he could tell. In order to share this love effectively, Peter realized that he should do it cautiously, by using the *fire* within him to warm those with whom he came into contact with, rather than burn them with his intense enthusiasm. From this philosophy, he knew that should not simply walk into Polydeck and begin *declaring God* by waving a Bible. Rather, Peter wanted to do all he could to create an environment filled with meaningful, as well as practical ways of *displaying God's love* and allowing this warm environment to cause other people to ask the question, "Why is he doing these acts of kindness?" Ultimately, he wanted them to seek and find the source of that love, Jesus the Christ

Reflection

In the Book of Daniel, Nebuchadnezzar was the king of Babylon. Nebuchadnezzar had built up a great nation and taken over many other nations in the process. He was obviously a shrewd king, and to those under his rule, his power was unlimited. In chapter three of Daniel the Bible states, "Nebuchadnezzar the king made an image of gold," and commanded that when the music was heard, everyone was to bow down and worship that image "that (the king) has set up." (Daniel 3:1-7 NASB)

In reading this passage, I have to wonder: What

did the image look like? Here was a man that had built an empire. In essence, he was the "CEO" of Babylon and his authority and power were not to be doubted or questioned. Look at who he was and what he had accomplished. The story tells us that Nebuchadnezzar's command was that this image was be "worshipped." But, what if we were to change the word to "glorified"? In many ways they mean the same thing. That which we glorify is that which we worship. So that brings us to a simple question: What is it that you glorify: in your home, in your workplace, in your heart?

If you were to construct an image at your workplace and command, everyone there to glorify that image, what would the image look like? If we were to ask your co-workers or employees, "What does your boss glorify in his life, and in the way he conducts his business?" If we were to ask your family, "What does your husband or wife, mother or father glorify in their lives, and in the way they conduct their home-life?

If I were to ask such questions, too often, I fear that if I were to go out to the yard, into the warehouse, or into the conference room, it would be clear, their monument would look just like "ME."

— CHAPTER 3 —

THE GHOST OF BUSINESS PAST, AND THE PROMISE OF BUSINESS FUTURE

How bad could things really be? Peter Freissle was a hard-charging business-man that had grown up in the family business. From an early age, Peter's dad—Man-fred—had introduced him to the family business with a work ethic that was "results oriented." In 1958, together with his German business partner, Helmut Rosenbusch, Peter's father started the business from scratch in a Johannesburg garage. As the business grew, Manfred and Helmut realized that God had placed them together and had blessed their business with success. Accordingly, the two men were committed to giving something back to God by supporting various Christian ministries. On numerous occasions, Peter had seen his Dad give thanks to God publicly during various company functions. Peter affectionately recalled, as a young man his father would take him to serve the less fortunate, as well as encourage Peter to get involved in Christian charities.

In 1978, Manfred and Dieter Egler—a lifetime friend—formed Polydeck. Over time, Peter took over the helm of Polydeck from Dieter and moved to South Carolina. When the business had thirty employees, Dieter was able to meet and greet almost every employee on a daily basis, and there was a sense of family. The business was run by being "strict but fair", mixed with compassion for employees with life problems; Dieter was affectionately known as the "Bear with a Golden Heart."

Peter felt like he had to prove himself to his father. With admiration and gratitude, he looked at what his dad and Dieter had built from scratch. Now, Peter felt like the "kid" taking over things, and he wanted to make sure everyone knew that he was every bit the businessman that his father was before him. Peter worked with a relentless drive to succeed and a work ethic that said, "My way is the right way. I am not to be questioned. Do it, do it right, do it fast, or get out." The company and the number of employees grew, but unfortunately, the working conditions began to deteriorate.

By many measures, Peter was doing a great job. Sales were up, margins were up, and the plant was growing fast. Peter was successful by business standards, except maybe in personnel. The Human Resources department was in constant turmoil. Employee turnover had hit an all time high, thirty-five percent. When there is exponential growth in a manufacturing business, there is a strong demand for workers; however, because of the turnover rate, Polydeck's source of new workers—the local temporary agency—was reluctant to send their people to Polydeck. The turnover rate of temporary personnel was so high, and so many complaints had been lodged against Polydeck that many of the local agencies refused to work with Polydeck. In the end, the temporary agencies were getting a bad reputation themselves by associating with Polydeck.

The pressure and stress was evident throughout the company, for Peter drove his leadership team unmercifully, and in turn, the leadership team drove their supervisors unmercifully. The supervisors showed no compassion for the line personnel and any supervisor unable or unwilling to demonstrate the same attitude toward the line workers "could leave, today!"

This German work ethic had two things going for it. First, the economy in the Spartanburg area was such that people simply needed the jobs. They worked there because at times there was no other place to work. Second, if you could make it at Polydeck, they paid you well. The wages and benefit package were at the top of the scale for the area, that was, if you could make it and if you could bear it.

Because of the high turnover rate, the busiest department at Polydeck was Human Resources, and they were criticized for not finding higher quality workers. It was as if any sign of compassion or consideration was seen as a sign of weakness, and weakness was not to be tolerated. As long as business success was to be measured by the bottom-line, there could be no question that Polydeck was on the right track.

A Different Metric?

During the retreat, when Peter realized that he had viewed God as a mere slice of his life, God showed Peter a different measure of business success. After that day, success became a much broader term. While financial success was certainly a major aspect of his business, Peter came to understand success as being measured in human values as well. One simple verse of Scripture delivered through the convicting power of the Holy Spirit was all it took. One simple verse that Peter had known for years, "In everything, do to others what you would have them do to you." (Matthew 7:12 NIV)

Wow! That brought Peter to his knees. After his return from the "silent retreat", he could barely stand to think of how he had treated those around him, especially his wife and all of his employees. God had removed the blinders from Peter's eyes, blinders that had prevented him from seeing that his "church life" had been separate from his home life and his business. For an hour or so on Sunday mornings, church seemed like the "right thing" to do with his family, but there was NO connection to what happened at Polydeck on Monday. With these blinders removed, he was moved and embarrassed to look back at the example that he had led, even encouraged, in his own business.

It was then that God laid another passage of Scripture on Peter's heart. "You shall love the Lord your God with all your heart, and with all your soul, and with all your strength, and with all your mind, and your neighbor as yourself." (Luke 10:27 NASB) In the Bible, this passage is followed by the simple question, "And who is my neighbor?" When Peter asked himself that question, the answer was undeniable, "My neighbor is everyone I encounter." If this was the case, what of those hundreds of neighbors that either worked for him, or were his suppliers or even his customers? Things must change. Things would change, and they would change, immediately.

The "silent retreat" was in June and during the following few months the changes in Peter, as well as the changes at Polydeck, were evident to everyone. Finally, the day of reckoning was at hand. There were annual company meetings scheduled for the week prior to the Thanksgiving holiday, and Peter knew that it was time to be held accountable for business past, and for business future. It was time to "come out of the closet" and if this feeling of gratitude and love for God was real, it was time to display his love publicly. Peter knew that this was a risky position, for once the declaration was made, there was "no going back", and he would be held accountable from that time forward.

Peter stood before the entire Polydeck workforce. "A couple of weekends ago I came into the plant by myself. As I walked around, what impacted me was how quiet everything was. None of you were here. The lights were not on, the machines were not running. And, it occurred to me, I don't even know how to turn the machines on. I realized that this plant, this business, is entirely dependent on the people that come in here every day to work."

"Polydeck is a success. We are growing. But I came to the realization that we are growing because of you."

Stunned silence followed this announcement.

The employees could not believe what they were hearing. Here is the "boss" that has been treating them like trash, treating them unmercifully, and now he turns around and tells them that the company success is because of the employees. How does that work?

Peter continued, "Things are going to change.

God has placed on my heart that you are what this company is all about, and I am promising you that from this point forward, I am going to care for you. We are going to put things in place to assure that you are treated as you should be, and that will help you to know that the people here at Polydeck are your family, and that they are a family that cares for you. I have realized that God will not ask me how much money we made but rather He will ask what we did with that money to please Him."

While Peter had a burning desire to share God's love with his employees, he wanted to be careful not to intimidate them or make anyone feel uncomfortable about the religious connotations related to his sentiments, especially knowing that his multi-cultural workforce represented many denominations of the Christian faith, other religions, and even no faith.

A month later, Peter followed up with a second meeting. As Peter introduced new employee benefits, part of the presentation was the sharing of "The Golden Rule." Peter shared, "The Bible says, 'Do to others as you would have them do to you.' Neighbors, from this point forward, this is my promise to you, that this company will be operated according to this principle. You all know where my office is and if any of you ever believe that they are not being treated according to this principle, or if you believe we have any business practice that does not conform to this principle, then I want you to come to my office and tell me. My promise to you is that we will make every effort to ensure that every decision made in this company will be made with this principle in mind."

There it was. In two meetings, over the course of thirty days, Peter had committed to the entire company that they would drastically change the way everyone was treated. Additionally, they would carefully examine every business practice to ensure that they were aligned with the biblical principle of the "Golden Rule." Peter had publicly promised a group of employees that had been treated without regard, that they would now be treated as "neighbors."

Accountability to his employees was a major step, but accountability within the walls of his home was even more of challenge. If God had really moved in Peter's heart, in that "everyone" was to be treated as a "neighbor", then this would have to extend beyond the safe walls of his own plant and office. That could be frightening and maybe even considered reckless. As a result of the new caring environment, business was terrific and thanks to the development of new programs, employee relations and operational procedures were improving on a daily basis.

Reflection

The most prolific writer in the New Testament was the apostle Paul. During his life, Paul started out as a tentmaker and went on to become a world-changing evangelist for the Good News of Jesus Christ, but he was not always that way.

Originally, Paul, named Saul, was educated in the best Jewish school of the time, and as a committed Jew, was zealous in his commitment to the Torah, as well as his persecution of "Christians." As a matter of fact, Saul was so committed to the persecution of Christians that he held the coats of the men that stoned one of Jesus' disciples—Stephen.

However, with all of the recognition and authority available to Saul, everything in his life changed with a single encounter with Jesus. In the ninth chapter of the Acts of the Apostles, Saul told his own story. He spoke of how he was still breathing threats, and was seeking letters to be taken to the synagogues in Damascus so that he might bring Christians in to be tried before the religious court. However, as Saul approached Damascus, he found himself face-to-face with a light that flashed so bright that it drove him to the ground; in fact, the light was so bright that he was struck blind. It was at that point that Saul heard a voice speaking to him from heaven; "Saul, Saul, why are you persecuting me?" The voice, Jesus, then instructed Saul to go into the city and there he would be told what to do.

From his experience on the Damascus Road, Saul was still blind, but with the help of his friends he was led into the city of Damascus. Once in the city of Damascus, Paul encountered Ananias. Now, Ananias informed Saul that he had been sent by the Lord so that Saul might regain his sight, and be filled with the Holy Spirit. Saul spent several days there in Damascus with the disciples, and IMME-DIATELY went out to proclaim Jesus in the synagogues (Acts 9:19–20). Saul had a single encounter, but it was an encounter that changed his life.

The Gospels tell many stories such as this. In the Gospel of Matthew we are told of Jesus walking by the Sea of Galilee when he saw two fishermen brothers, Simon Peter and Andrew. After a single simple encounter with Jesus, the Scripture tells that the two fishermen left their nets and followed Him.

As Jesus walked on from there He came across two other brothers, James and John, working in their fishing boat along with their father Zebedee. Again, after another single encounter, these men left their boat, as well as their father, and followed Jesus.

Sometimes it may require a blinding light. Other times all it required was a simple "Follow me, and I will make you fishers of men." Either way, a true encounter with Jesus Christ, the Master of the Universe, will result in the person seeing the world through new eyes. Tent-building may be all you know. Fishing may be your life's work, but if it is not done for the sake of, and to the glory of Jesus Christ, is there any value to the work?

—Chapter 4—

Birth of a Business Card

Things were changing fast at Polydeck. At first, because of the years of heavy-handedness by management at all levels of the business; the employees were skeptical about the new policy of "Do unto others…" While it certainly sounded like a good idea to everyone on the manufacturing floor, it would require a restructuring, as well as a retraining of the management team. Peter's story had sounded good, and the second meeting pleasantly surprised them, but a lasting change of attitude was difficult for the employees to grasp. The employees understood that numbers, not relationships, controlled business and everyone was unsure of what would take place if Polydeck's numbers were to drop or become unstable. Simply, the employees were afraid that the old familiar hammer would be coming back down.

Things were also changing fast with Peter. He was committed to change in his personal life as well as his business, and he set out to learn everything he could about doing business in this "new way." Suddenly, Peter discovered that he had a passion for caring for his employees, as well as a passion for allowing his workplace to be the "salt and light" that showed people what Jesus Christ had done in his life; likewise, Peter understood that he must be wise in how he went about being "salt and light." Polydeck was a multicultural workplace, and their customer base was certainly multicultural. How could he "live out his faith" for his "neighbors", while being careful not to offend or to violate the law?

Surprisingly, he found that there were already business people out there that were committed to this same mission. Peter read everything he could get his hands on about Jesus in the workplace and talked with business people across the nation for ideas. During the search, Peter came across a book entitled *A Light Shines in Babylon*, by Buck Jacobs. Jacobs's book was revolutionary thinking for Peter. In the book, Jacobs proposed three basic lessons–– You Have a Holy Calling, Your Work is Your Ministry, and Working Your Ministry.

That was it! For Peter it was now clear. There was no question that he had a holy calling and he now recognized that work was his ministry. The next steps were to change his policies, procedures, and perhaps his people's attitudes to "work His ministry."

As Peter considered his new position, he realized there were many things that he could do at Polydeck that would make it a better, more comfortable, workplace. If Polydeck was really his ministry, and his ministry was to be to "his neighbors", and if "his neighbors" included everyone, then Peter knew that he would have to reach further than the changes within the walls of his company. What could he do that would communicate to everyone he came into contact with, that is, his employees, his customers, and the world, that he is committed to honoring God in everything he does?

Peter realized that he needed to have a statement that he could write down and share. This statement must explain what the values and purpose of the "new" Polydeck were to be. In Peter's mind, there were two options, either create this statement on your own or create it in collaboration with the key players of his team. After prayerful consideration, Peter chose to make it a team effort. He gathered his team together and began to share his heart and vision for the business. While some participated with caution and skepticism, others gave ideas and recommendations, and after a few hours of debate and consideration, the Polydeck Core Value statement was born. Working through the process as a group allowed the team generate consensus, as well as establish a feeling of ownership to the established principals.

The Sales Meeting

Peter walked into the sales meeting with a smile on his face and his arms full of boxes. The entire Polydeck sales team was there, and business had been good, so no one was too surprised that Peter was in a good mood. Many of the sales team members had been present at the two meetings in the fall when Peter had declared that there were going to be changes at Polydeck. One thing they had to admit was that Peter had been faithful to his promise for change. The changes had been remarkable. The treatment and attitudes at the corporate office were like a different company, and the interaction between the executive team and the sales staff was unbelievable. Polydeck had become a great place to work. The team in operations was getting along with the sales team; prior to the change, this was unheard of. Sales was working hard to provide all specifications and information needed so that the Production team could get their job done on time and in full.

The sales meeting was a success, for the reports had been good and encouraging. With the improved attitudes and communication throughout the company, warranty claims, as well as rework had decreased, and market reports showed an increase. In fact, everyone was gearing up for a great year. Then, it was time for Peter's closing remarks, "Gentlemen, I am excited about the past year, and encouraged for the coming year. However, I am even more excited about something that I have to share with you. We all have new business cards." Peter then handed each Sales Engineer a box of their new cards.

What is the big deal, new business cards? So what? That was, until they saw their new cards. The front of the cards was pretty much the same as it had been in year's past—standard business cards with the company logo and contact information. The cards were nicely done, with three-color artwork on the front of each card; however, on the back of each card was printed the "Polydeck Mission Statement." Putting the Mission Statement on the business cards made a strong statement to a high standard.

POLYDECK MISSION STATEMENT

To be the innovative leader in the modular screen media industry by partnering with our customers and focusing on:

- A proactive Research and Development program;
- Uncompromising quality standards;
- Guaranteed performance and unrivaled customer satisfaction through superior service and after-sales support.

CORE VALUES

We are a company grounded in Christian values of honesty, integrity, respect, kindness and a sense of social responsibility. We strive to honor God in all we do. This is reflected in how we conduct our business and how we care for our employees – our greatest asset.

Even with all the artwork, it was the Core Values that got everyone's attention. Can we really say that "We are a company grounded in Christian values…"? Is it wise or safe to say that we "strive to honor God" in our business? Should we be more careful about mixing religion and business? Are we discriminating? If not, certainly, we are alienating others. (Polydeck does business around the world, in various cultural settings and with people of other religions.)

One of the Sales Engineers asked Peter, "Are you sure you want to do this? I can think of a few of my customers right now that this will surely offend. And if we offend them, we are going to lose their business. Is this a wise business move?"

Another asked, "I'm sure this is going to cost us business. And there is no one around here that pushes harder for sales than you do. When we come back and we have either lost a customer, or failed to make a sale, and we are sure that it has to do with this card you have given us, what are you going to say? Quite frankly, conditions around here were just starting to improve, and now I fear you are putting us into a position that there could be a significant loss to the company, and a significant commission loss to me, personally. Are you going to stand behind me when I lose a sale because of this card?"

Peter responded, "Gentlemen, you are all familiar with our Mission Statement and there is nothing new there, except for our commitment to it. Our Mission Statement tells our employees and the world what we do as a business. But it is our Core Values that tell our employees and the world <u>how</u> and <u>why</u> we do our business. These Core Values are the "how" and "why" of Polydeck. These Core Values are why I am here, and these Core Values will reflect everything I have to do with this business. In addition, as Sales Engineers for Polydeck, you are my representatives to our customers and the world, and as my representatives, you will reflect these Core Values in everything you do concerning Polydeck. And, as you honor and reflect this Mission Statement and these Core Values, I will provide every bit of support I possibly can."

"I truly believe that if we are doing everything we can to align ourselves personally and professionally with this Mission Statement and these Core Values, and we lose a customer, then that is a customer that I am prepared to live without. I promise to support you in that."

When Peter finished speaking, the room was quiet. The employees sitting before him began to like the ideas he had presented, but were not sure how it would work out. Some were thinking about specific customers, about using the old cards with some customers and the new ones with other customers. Some of the employees simply wondered if Peter had lost his mind.

As they sat and read, and reread the card, many made an interesting observation. There was nothing on the card about Polydeck's Christian expectations of their customers or even their employees. All of the expectations were directed to how Polydeck would perform. The Core Values was a simple statement as to how Polydeck would treat others.

Reflection

As Peter realized that "his work was his ministry", he knew that part of "being in ministry" was making a clear statement about Jesus Christ. There is a passage in the Gospel of Matthew that is most often used when referring to someone that has "gone down front" at their local church. That is, an individual that has made a public profession of their faith in Jesus Christ, "Everyone therefore who shall confess Me before men, I will also confess him before My Father who is in heaven" (Matthew 10:32).

Jesus made this statement after he had chosen the twelve disciples, and as He was preparing to send them out. Jesus chose these twelve men as the original ambassadors to go out into the world and spread the Good News of Jesus Christ. While Jesus makes the statement directly to those twelve men, the application is to all believers, of all times. Publically, when we profess the name of Jesus Christ,

Jesus Himself will profess us to the Father. (Matthew 10:32 NASB)

How wonderful is that? Do you fear taking the risk? Are you afraid of the impact that a public profession might have on your business? Every businessperson is familiar with the term Return on Investment (ROI). What greater ROI could there possibly be than to have Christ Himself speaking to the Father on our behalf? At that point, the challenge is for us to determine whether we believe that God is the Master of the Universe. Is God in control? Or, do I still believe that I should keep my business separate from my spiritual life?

You can ask the question in Sunday school classes and church services on any given Sunday, "Can God take you out of your job/business?" Invariably, the majority of individuals sitting around you will agree that God can take us out of our job or close our business in a moment. God is all-powerful; God is omnipotent!

Now, ask that same group, if they believe that God can take you out of your job or business, do you believe that God put you in your job or business? Sadly, the agreement does not come as quickly. Many of us believe that we are where we are because we earned it or because of something that we have done. We deserve it! We went to school, studied hard, "paid our dues" in the workplace. We worked hard for this job and this position; beat out everyone else in the process, and we are proud of where we are. Do we really believe that we are that much smarter than everyone else is? Is it possible that we worked that much harder than the rest of the pack in the job market?

In the book *A Light Shines Bright in Babylon*, Buck Jacobs stated the following prayer, "Dear God I don't believe that you own my business. I created it, I worked to build it and it is mine. So, in order to settle this issue of ownership once and for all, God, I challenge you to take away all of my business that is Yours and leave me with what is mine."

The Bible offers us much evidence that God is in control, and that the workings of man fit within that control. Consider Proverbs 19:21, "Many are the plans in a person's heart, but it is the Lord's purpose that prevails." Perhaps more clear Scriptural support that focuses our ministry in the workplace is found in Colossians 1:16, where the writer stated, "For in Him all things were created; things in heaven and on earth, visible and invisible, whether thrones or powers or rulers or authorities; all things have been created through him and for him."

You have likely been obedient in your study and hard work. You have "paid your dues." But, it is by

God's grace, and for God's glory, that you are where you are in the workplace. That being said, if you are where you are by God's grace, and if Jesus Christ Himself professes you before the Father, isn't it only right that you share with others as to who is really responsible for your achievements?

— CHAPTER 5—

RUBBER MEETS THE ROAD

The decision had been made; Peter had new business cards for the entire sales team, including himself. The Mission Statement and the Core Values were clearly printed on the back of the new business cards. Peter suspected that many, if not all of the sales team had kept their old cards and planned to use the new cards only if they felt that they would be accepted. While Peter understood their reluctance, he believed that this was what God desired from him, and that this is what God desired from Polydeck.

To this end, Peter knew that he would have to lead by example; therefore, today was the day that the rubber would meet the road. At the time, Peter was in Asia and was scheduled for a meeting with the manager of one of the largest mines in that part of the world. Polydeck had a small part of this company's business and they were examining ways to enhance their relationship with the mining company; thus increasing their contracts. Aseph—the manager of the company—as well as many within the operation, was Muslim. Now, there was a fear that the new Business Card might lose what business they had with the mine.

As Peter was introduced to Aseph, the two men exchanged greetings and business cards, and everything started out very cordial between them. While

Peter was given a complete tour of the facility, he held his breath for the inevitable moment, when Aseph would read the business card. The "elephant in the living room" had to be addressed at some point. The issue was just too major to be overlooked. Toward the end of the afternoon, Aseph finally addressed the issue.

"You know, I have read your business card, front and back."

"Oh, really?"

"Yes, I have read it, and I want you to know that I respect you for doing what you have done. The values that you have printed there are honorable values. They are the same values that I live by, and most of my Muslim brethren try to live by. I do not agree with some aspects of your faith; for example, while we believe that Jesus was a man, we do not believe that He was the Son of God. I do believe that we pray to the same God and I support what you are doing. It tells me a lot about you and about your company." As Aseph and Peter continued chatting, they discussed their families and their different faiths. As the two men explored the many things that they had in common, both Peter and Aseph came to respect each other.

Thank God for this response. Aseph had been more than kind, and Peter appreciated his support, but he still had to meet with the other principles of the company. Being kind to Peter and doing business with him might be two different things. A company with several managers that were Muslim doing business with an overtly Christian company might be too much to ask.

The following day was the big meeting. Peter made his presentation to the senior management team and everything seemed to go well. Then it was time to get down to the hard part of the meeting. Finally, the CEO spoke, "Aseph, you have spent time with Peter, and you have been using a bit of his product for some time. Tell us what you think."

"You are correct; we have been working with Polydeck, but on a limited basis. Our experience, however, has been very good. We have found their product to be high quality, and even more, their product support has been tremendous. I'm very impressed."

"Are you impressed enough to endorse this company for the entire operation?"

"Absolutely, I believe in this company. I believe in what they stand for. They have treated us fairly in all aspects of our dealings, and we desire to work with them."

"Good. Mr. Freissle, thank you for your time. Allow us some time to discuss the matter, and we will get back with you shortly."

Well, that was it. Peter had done his best, and he had been faithful to what he believed God would have him do. They had a great product and good history with the company. Going in, Polydeck had about 30% of the mining company's business and Peter was hoping, no, he was praying for the percentage to increase to 50%. Actually, he had at first been praying that they wouldn't lose the company's business. But now things seemed brighter and Peter sensed that Polydeck just might get the 50% he was praying for.

True to their word, a follow-up meeting was scheduled. "Mr. Freissle, we have looked closely at your product, as well as the products of some of your competitors, and we have spent a great deal of time discussing possibilities with our senior managers."

"Originally, I know you came here with the hope of increasing your contract with our company, and possibly increasing it to as much as 50%; however, based on the feedback from Aseph and his team, we have decided that we are not going to give you 50%." Peter's heart sank.

"We have a contract here offering you 100% of our business. There is one other important element of this contract. We would like to offer you 100% of our business, for the life of the mine."

Surely, Peter did not hear the CEO correctly. He knew that his product was high quality, but 100% of the business? Any mine is going to spread their business somewhat, just to keep their options open. Did he really hear this right? For the life of the mine? This type of contract was unheard of in Peter's business. This is not possible.

But it was; and it is. Yes, Peter did hear the terms of the contract correctly. Peter wondered if this was a reward from God for being faithful; or, was it just good business on the part of the Asian company, or both? Again, one may ask, "Is this a co-Incidence, or is this a God-incidence"? There was no doubt in Peter's mind. Either way, Peter returned from Asia ready to dispel the fears of his sales team. Peter knew that not every sales call was going to turn out like this one, but he knew that God had confirmed to him that he was to follow that original call, and follow it completely. Peter's return to Spartanburg was interesting, because as Peter recounted the story to the VP of Sales and the sales team, excitement was followed by wonder, and the wonder was followed by confidence.

Reflection

There are cynics that see the "sign of the fish" emblem on a work truck or business card, and immediately think that this person or company is using this emblem as a way to draw business, possibly. Here in the United States it is hard to believe that anyone would be so offended by a Christian emblem that they would not do business with a company because of such a declaration. As we trade in the global market and as the United States continues to become even more multi-cultural, there are certainly both countries and companies that would refuse to do business strictly based on religious beliefs.

That being said, are you sure that you want to make a public declaration that you are a Christian? In addition, if so, what is your purpose in that declaration? Are you displaying "the fish" to draw attention with the hope of doing business with other Christians? On the other hand, are you declaring, "I am a Christian, and as such, I will conduct my business with you as indicated in the Epistle of James, with wisdom, humility, and a dependence on God."

Of course, that is a tall order. In the Epistle of James the author stated, "For where jealousy and selfish ambition exist, there is disorder and every evil thing. But the wisdom from above is first pure, then peaceable, gentle, reasonable, full of mercy and good fruits, unwavering, without hypocrisy. And the seed whose fruit is righteousness is sown in peace by those who make peace." (James 3:16-18 NASB)

When we are working with clients or customers that practice these attributes, it is easy for us to return them. Unfortunately, not everyone we work with is going to be concerned with peace, gentleness, or mercy. Sometimes we might have to work with people that are only concerned with coming out on top, regardless of the circumstance. Sometimes we might encounter people that discriminate against us because of our faith. Flip over a few pages to 1 Peter 2:20 and to see how this author would have you respond, "For what credit is there if, when you sin and are harshly treated, you endure it with patience? But if when you do what is right and suffer for it you patiently endure it, this finds favor with God."

CHAPTER 6

THERE'S GOING TO BE A BARBEQUE, AND YOU'RE INVITED

"They are going to chew you up and spit you out." That was David's counsel to Peter for the big meeting on the following day. David had a meeting with the same people earlier in the day and that was what happened to him.

A few months earlier, Polydeck had sold a large job to a mine in New Jersey. As always, exact specifications must be provided by the mine, and strict adherence by Polydeck was guaranteed, but in this particular case something had gone wrong. There was an error in the specifications and it resulted in the loss of $750,000 of raw material at the mine. In addition, there were losses in production time, refitting, and resourcing. The list was growing and the potential loss was catastrophic. Threat of a lawsuit was on the table and the situation was getting to a critical point.

David went to New Jersey prepared for the initial meeting. In the past David had dealt with the Vice President of Operations, and they had a good working rapport. As David traveled to New Jersey, he assumed that he would get together with the VP and hash out a solution, thus putting the incident behind them.

Nothing could have been further from the truth. As David walked into the meeting, he was surprised to see the VP of Operations, President of the company, several other company representatives, and the company's legal counsel. There were twelve representatives from the mine present at the meeting and one of him. As David entered the conference room, he knew that this was not going to be a pleasant meeting.

The introductions were brief, and the president began to speak. Clearly, he was in a hostile frame of mind. The president accused Polydeck of messing up. His company had provided the correct specifications and information, and Polydeck had obviously messed up the fabrication, as well as the installation of their equipment. According to the President, this whole disaster was the fault of Polydeck and he wanted the losses paid. He wanted the problem corrected, and he wanted it done "RIGHT NOW!"

David had been in the business for a long time and over the years he had dealt with his share of disgruntled customers, but this time it was different. There was no way he had the authority to give this customer what he wanted, and even if he had the authority, he did not believe that Polydeck was at fault.

Even more difficult than the meeting was the decision that David had to make next. As a Sales Engineer, how would it look for him to call the boss to help him out? In all his years in sales, and certainly in all his years at Polydeck, David had never experienced a dilemma in which he felt so powerless. The decision was painful, but necessary. He needed help, and he needed it immediately. David put in a call to Peter and shared his concerns. That was the call that brought Peter up for this second meeting.

The next day, Peter and David entered the boardroom and were faced with the same formidable twelve from the day before. Introductions were briefer at this meeting and immediately the President of the mine launched into his diatribe of Polydeck's errors and responsibility in the matter. He communicated that Polydeck was responsible for over $1,000,000 in losses and damages, and he expected Polydeck to fix "their" problem, as well as pay the mine for their accumulating losses.

Finally, it was Peter's turn to speak, and he knew exactly where he must start: with TRUTH. Peter began by handing one of his business cards to everyone on the other side of the table. Then, he then asked that everyone read the back of the business card—Polydeck's Mission Statement and Core Values. After a brief pause, Peter spoke directly to the President, "Sir, I wanted you to first know the Core Values of our company. I want you to know exactly where I am coming from, how I will conduct our end of this meeting, how we will behave, and what principles I will use to come to a resolution in this matter."

The president picked up Peter's card, read it again, indignantly flung it to the table, and turned his chair to stare out the window. After a few moments he turned back to the table, read the business card a third time, again indignantly flung the card to the table, and again turned his chair to stare out the window. Each time the president stared out the window, Peter braced for attack. Each time the livid executive read the card, Peter felt more like a lamb being led to slaughter. The tension in the room was rising exponentially and all eyes were on the president.

In the weeks preceding the meeting, Polydeck's position had been made clear to the mining company. Everyone in the room knew that Polydeck maintained that the project had been performed according to the specifications that they had been provided. The problem was that everyone knew that the mine representatives, as well as their president, had come to the meeting with one thing in mind, make Polydeck pay.

The president began to speak in a surprisingly calm tone that suggested a change was taking place.

"I have these same values. I believe we need a brief recess for me to meet with our people." At that point the president, along with his entourage, arose and left the room. A few minutes later the entire group returned to the board room. The president began to speak again. "I have just spoken with our Plant Manager and we realize that we have some culpability on our side of the table. Also, I realize that this issue is not near as complex as we had at first supposed. Tell me what you and Polydeck can do to help us resolve this matter."

What? Was this the same president and group that the day before had verbally crushed the Polydeck sales engineer? In this meeting they had come at Peter with everything they had, including the promise of a lawsuit. Now, they were politely and humbly asking for help? In a matter of a few minutes, the barbeque had turned into a picnic. Originally, Peter and David were the main course, but were now favored guests and partners. In less than half an hour, solutions were discovered and issues were resolved. At the end of the meeting the president invited Peter to return to the mine at a later date as his guest.

What could possibly have happened? Cooler heads prevailed? Not likely, there were no cool heads. The mine representatives had been out for blood, and Peter and David were simply hoping to come away with no open wounds. What happened could only have been one thing. The convictions stated on The Business Card had been tested, and Peter and David had passed. When faced with an extremely difficult situation the Core Values had won the day. The very Holy Spirit that had guided them in the writing of the Core Values, and had encouraged them in the printing of the Core Values on their business cards, had taken control of the meeting.

They had more than won the day; they had won over. The representatives from the mine had first realized that you cannot fight with someone that will not fight back, but even more had realized that they had no fight with someone that was steered by the Christian values of honesty, integrity, and respect.

Everyone had been geared up for a barbeque, but the "sacrificial lamb" had been protected. Sometimes even when the barbeque is canceled, you get to enjoy dessert. This potentially disastrous experience was a significant marker for David. David had worked with Peter for several years, and valued both their professional and personal relationship. When David shares the story of The Business Card and the confrontation at the New Jersey mine, he points out that his working relationship with Peter started long before Peter's awakening and transformation. David has seen Peter in all sorts of business situations, when times were good and when times were not so good. Because of this, David was not sure how Peter was going to handle being "the main course at the barbeque." There were a couple of possible responses to the verbal assault that he had experienced the day before.

The response that David witnessed was a response of humility. It was a response of a man that knew that Jesus is the Master of the Universe, and that Jesus was the Master of that meeting. It was a response of a man that knew that printing business cards was inexpensive and easy, but living a life that was committed to the Core Values stated thereon, was essential. To do otherwise was not only to lie to his customers and his employees, but to lie to the very God that had given him his life and this business.

The New Jersey experience was a turning point for David. Like many of the sales staff, he had pushed back a bit at the risk, even exposure, of making such a bold statement on their business cards. "Does this mean regardless of the situation?" "Does this mean regardless of the cost?" "Will Peter really back us up if and when we are challenged?"

In this most hostile of situations, Peter did not back David up; Peter led the charge. David's boss, the company president, had stated clearly and convincingly, that this was how he and Polydeck would conduct their business under any and all circumstances.

David left New Jersey that day no longer carrying a business card that he feared as a liability. He left New Jersey carrying "The Business Card" that he knew to be an asset, a statement of who he was and who he represented. David got to witness an unbelievable event. To this day he cannot fully explain it, yet he enthusiastically shares this "war story" with his fellow salesmen and encourages them to support the Core Value statement on the back of their business card.

As Peter reflects back on this memorable event, it still amazes him how the power of the Holy Spirit was so clearly evident that it made an indelible mark on all those in the board room that day, one that was unbelievable––real and undeniable. To Peter, this event was undeniable evidence of the impact of a few simple words of Truth on the back of a business card, mixed with *conviction* and trust in the life altering power of the Master of the Universe.

Reflection

Returning to the Book of Daniel, you will recall that Nebuchadnezzar was the king of Babylon. Babylon was a great nation and had achieved greatness through conquering adjacent nations. In the process they have taken many slaves, including three young Jewish men named Shadrach, Meshach, and Abednego.

In the third chapter of Daniel, the story was told of how Nebuchadnezzar passed a law requiring everyone to bow down and worship a god that he had constructed. Failure to bow down and worship meant that the offender would be thrown into the furnace of blazing fire. Shadrach, Meshach, and Abednego had grown up as Jews, and they knew the Word of God. By knowing the Word of God, they knew the will of God and they knew that God would not have them bow down an idol, would not have them submit to an ungodly order, even to save their own lives.

In Daniel 3:15, they were told a second time that refusal to bow—to submit—would result in their destruction. Their answer was clear, "If it be so, our God whom we serve is able to deliver us from the furnace of blazing fire…But even if He does not, let it be known to you, O king, that we are not going to serve your gods or worship the golden image you have set up."

I am sure that Shadrach, Meshach, and Abednego had several possible resolutions in mind. God could change the king's heart and the king could forgive them, and allow them to go on their way. God could change the king's heart, and he could choose an alternate punishment, less severe. God could not intervene and they could be thrown in to the blazing fire, and be burned up. The faith and courage of Shadrach, Meshach, and Abednego did not rest on knowing the eventual outcome. Their faith and courage rested on knowing that God was able to deliver them, and whatever the outcome, they were in God's hands.

Business decisions are often complex and complicated. Sometimes we are faced with deciding between several of the "most right" options. Frequently decisions boil down simply to what is the right thing to do and what is not.

Following the example of these three young men, we must know that once we determine God's will in our life and our work we must move on knowing that God wants HIS best for us. Regardless of the circumstance, we are in His hands. If we truly trust that we are in God's hands, while the battle may rage, our decision is clear. Continuing in this same chapter of Daniel, we find that the three men were thrown into the blazing fire, but something odd happened. They were not burned up, but were seen to be "walking about" in the midst of the fire.

While the will of the king had been carried out, the God of the Universe—the real King—had intervened in the lives of these three men. God intervened in a way that they could never have imagined, for God alone received the glory. An interesting point was that the chapter ended with," Then the king caused Shadrach, Meshach, and Abednego to prosper in the province of Babylon."

— CHAPTER 7—

WHAT HAPPENS
IN VEGAS...

Polydeck is a manufacturer of screen media used specifically for mines and quarries. As many industries, the mining industry has an international convention, so large that it is only held every three years and it is billed as "the world's largest and most comprehensive exposition dedicated to mining." What a great opportunity for the Polydeck sales department to get in front of potential customers from mines around the world. For most of the Sales Engineers at Polydeck this was not a new experience. They had been to the Las Vegas convention many times.

The relationships established and maintained at this show could make or break Polydeck, and they could certainly define a career for any of the Sales Engineers. While Polydeck was an industry leader in quality and application of their product, everyone knows that the first step in sales is to establish relationships. Regardless of the industry or product, relationship is the deciding factor in many sales. With that in mind Polydeck, as well as their competition, would always hit Las Vegas with a mission and a strategy. Do whatever it takes and spend whatever is necessary to entertain the various mine representatives. As one can imagine, in Las Vegas "whatever it takes" is a broad statement that might include all sorts of substance abuse and debauchery.

In years past there were no boundaries, "What happened in Vegas, stayed in Vegas." Establish the relationship, get the appointment; thus get the deal. Basically, your goal would be to out-schmooze the competition.

That was the strategy of the "old Polydeck." What about now, what about the "new Polydeck". For weeks prior to the show, Peter had been burdened about its outcome, for he knew how God had spoken to him and how his heart had changed. Peter had concrete evidence of God's protection and blessing through the conviction to strive for adherence to the Core Values. This would be different, because it included the entire sales team, and they had been doing business the Vegas-way for years. As Peter thought through the possibilities, he realized that he could personally maintain his adherence to the Core Values, and at the same time allow his sales team to "use their best judgment." This was not one sale he was talking about, but what happened at this conference would set the course for the entire year.

Clearly, there was a small segment of the buying market that might agree with the Core Values and would appreciate his stand; but this was their one opportunity to visit with virtually every client and potential customer from around the world. Peter knew this would be a defining moment for Polydeck. The choices were business as usual and continue to flourish and grow as a company and industry leader, or take a huge risk and possibly experience tremendous loss in sales. Loss in sales would translate into personal income loss for each of his sales team, which would undoubtedly result in Peter losing some of his key sales people. Integrity is a huge word. It is often defined as "doing what is right, when no one is looking." A more difficult definition is "doing what is right, regardless of the cost."

The night before the show Peter met with his sales team, "Gentlemen, while you are here in Las Vegas, you represent Polydeck and as such, you represent our Core Values. You need to know that should you choose to violate these Core Values there will be significant consequences for you personally, and for our company." One Sales Engineer replied, "Peter, you know that there are several customers coming from around the world that do not share these values, and substantial contracts and business hangs in the balance for us entertaining them here in Las Vegas. Are you okay with the fact that if we choose to go down this path, we might lose their business?"

Peter replied, "This is where the rubber meets the road. This is where I must stand up for what I truly believe. When you are with these customers, you are representing Polydeck and when you are representing Polydeck you are representing me personally. I cannot allow, no, I will not allow anyone here to represent me in any way other than what we have put on the back of our business cards. If we live those values and we lose that business, then I do not want that business. If that is what it takes to get that business, they need to go elsewhere."

In addition, "I want you to all know that you are not only here as Polydeck employees. You are here as husbands and fathers. And it is essential that you remember when you are out there over the next few days that you are representing yourself, as well as Polydeck. You are representing to the world what you consider to be a husband. Would you be proud to share the price you have paid for a particular contract before your wife?" What happens in Vegas does not stay in Vegas. What happens in Vegas, or Dallas, or Brazil, or Indonesia, defines who you are. Integrity does not waver with circumstance. Harry Truman said, "Do right, and risk the consequences."

Simple, but true. As a leader, it is important that you understand that invariably you will be defined by your lowest mark. Regardless of the rationalization, a breech in integrity speaks clearly to those that follow you, "He is a fine leader, a great man, who will do whatever is necessary to get the job done." This may sound good, but what is the cost? What does it really mean to "get the job done?"

Peter's decision was made easy. The behavior of the Sales Engineers reflected back on Peter as the President and CEO of Polydeck. By Peter understanding that God owned his business, he realized that his behavior would reflect back on THE OWNER. A clear understanding of mission (Mission Statement) and values (Core Values) simplified the process.

As Peter reflects on this issue, he often marvels that through defining and communicating the Core Values, they not only have become the "Invisible hand", that guides the "how and why" of the business, but they hold each person accountable to these values on both a personal and social level. The Core Values have become the "bar" by which everything and everyone is measured. Sales and profit are important to any business, but if the true mission is to glorify God, then sales and profits are secondary, possibly even a by-product.

In some ways, decisions such as these are complex because they might impact your spiritual life and your business/financial life. The impact on the spiritual life is immediate, for the peace that comes with obedience is undeniable and often overwhelming. The financial impact is measured later, for you often do not know whether you have lost certain business. You can always measures gains or losses in sales and revenue. Maybe it was just a good economic year for mining, or maybe it was just good luck. Maybe it was a result of the Sales Engineers working harder and smarter, knowing that they did not have one of their "normal" sales tools. Or, maybe it was God's blessing on the Sales Engineers and Polydeck for their obedience. It's impossible to know, but what we do know is that sales stemming from the Las Vegas convention that year set new records for Polydeck. Relationships were formed based on sound business practices and quality materials, not on paid visits to strip clubs.

In addition, the spouses of the Sales Engineers can now take great comfort in knowing that their husbands are not expected to cross a line of integrity in their marriage. Instead, they are being encouraged and supported as they walk the "narrow path."

Reflection

Earlier we looked at the story of Daniel, Nebuchadnezzar, and Shadrach, Meshach and Abednego. When Nebuchadnezzar, king of Babylon, defeated Judah, he transported many of the captives to his homeland and ordered that the smartest, best-looking, and wisest of the youths of Judah be brought to work in his court. Nebuchadnezzar's intent was two-fold. First, he would have excellent service from the best and the brightest slaves. Second, he sought to assimilate these young men into his culture, insuring their full allegiance.

As with any favored position, there were certain benefits granted to these young men, including daily rations from the king's choice food and drink, as well as the best education. The benefits presented a major problem for Daniel and his friends. The food and drink of Nebuchadnezzar was a direct violation of the biblical food standards of these young Jewish men. Jewish law included strict food standards to maintain holiness and to insure that the people of Israel were easily recognized as being distinctly different. They were to be different in ways that would be clear to anyone observing them.

Having grown up in Jerusalem, these young men were familiar with both the Levitical law and the purposes stated in Deuteronomy. They knew right from wrong.

In Daniel 1:8–21, young Daniel had made up his mind that he would not defile himself by partaking of the king's food and drink. Daniel went to the commander of the officials, their "supervisor", and asked permission not to eat the king's food, but to be given food that did not violate biblical standards.

He knew that the king had provided this food, knowing that if his servants were well fed that they would perform better, and serve him better. Daniel offered a challenge to the commander. "Please test your servants for ten days, and let us be given some vegetables to eat and water to drink. Then let our appearance be observed in your presence, and the appearance of the youths who are eating the king's choice food; and deal with your servants according to what you see."

The results of this risky challenge were given in verses 15–16, "And at the end of ten days their appearance seemed better and they were [healthier] than all the youths who had been eating the king's choice food. So the overseer continued to withhold their choice food and the wine they were to drink, and kept giving them vegetables."

In our various workplaces we are challenged to adjust our standards to our culture, our industry, or our company, knowing all the while that this standard is less than what God would ask of us. What could be wrong? The salesmen are closing deals, business is doing well, or our friends are good people that we enjoy being with. After all, we are not completely giving in; we are merely compromising.

What God asks of us is clear. Especially, as Christians in the workplace, we are to be different. We are to be distinctly different. Set aside for holiness.

Daniel's message went a step further. When Daniel and his friends maintained God's standard, the Scripture stated, "Their appearance seemed better" than the others when maintaining God's standard. Even more, in verse 20 of the Scripture, it states that "he (the King) found them ten times better than all the (others)…" In the workplace, our goal should not be to merely survive while maintaining God's standard. Our goal should be to "(perform) better" because of God's standard.

You see, when Daniel and his friends requested something different to eat, the difference between them and the rest of the servants became obvious. After the trial period, when the commander compared Daniel and his friends to the other servants, the difference was obvious. When your co-workers, employees, customers, community, look at you, is the difference obvious?

—CHAPTER 8—

PREPARE FOR BATTLE

Beginning in 2006, each month the Caring Committee brings in a local non-profit organization to see what Polydeck can do to help them. As a matter of policy, a set percentage of Polydeck's revenues (not profits) are set aside to contribute to local organizations. They believe that this is a step in living out their faith in the community and sharing the resources that God has blessed and entrusted them with.

There in the boardroom, the young man from Campus Crusade had just shared how he had given his life to Christ and how he trusted Christ in even the most difficult of times. Just then there was a knock on the door. Out of respect for the visiting organization, the committee worked hard to keep from being disturbed during their monthly meeting. This must be serious. Peter's Administrative Assistant tells him that he needs to come out of the meeting, and he needs to come out "right now." There is an officer of the court there and he has asked to speak specifically with Peter. Polydeck, as well as Peter, were being sued.

Several months before Peter had been approached by a major competitor that expressed a desire to buy Polydeck. When Peter informed the competitor that he was not interested, the mood of the meeting changed. Peter was a second-generation business owner that had grown up in this company. In addition, Peter was looking forward to the day when he could teach his children the business, and eventually work side-by-side with them. This threat of a takeover did not sit too well with Peter.

After months of rejecting the competitors' offers, Polydeck was now being sued by the wishful competitor for patent infringement. This could not be possible. There was no way that Polydeck had violated any laws, and they certainly had not infringed on any existing patents, but Peter and Polydeck soon found out that in the court system, being right and proving right were two different things. It was going to cost a fortune to defend against the charges, but the only other option was to give in and sell the company.

This was as difficult a situation as Peter had ever encountered. Although Peter was confident that he and Polydeck were in the right, their foe was the proverbial eight-hundred pound gorilla. This was truly a "David and Goliath" battle. The suing party appeared to have unlimited resources.

Another Core Value decision had to be made. Do we adhere relentlessly to the Christian values of honesty and integrity and risk everything? Do we cave in to fraud and manipulation? Caving in would result in Peter selling the company and receiving a respectable sum of money, but it would also result in Peter sacrificing his integrity.

Once again Peter was put in the position of determining whether he was completely dedicated to the Core Values, or whether they are a guide. Peter prayed for God's guidance. This was not a decision that would impact only Peter; this was a decision that would impact the jobs of everyone at Polydeck. In prayer, God had two answers for Peter. First, "Peter, why do you think that of all the times these papers could have been delivered, they were delivered while you were in the middle of doing MY work?" And the second came in the small chapel (affectionately known at Polydeck as the Boss's office) that had been built in the center of the Polydeck office complex.

As Peter prayed, a picture in the chapel caught his eye. Although he had seen this picture many times, suddenly, God's answer was revealed. Depicted in the picture was Jesus walking on the water, hands outstretched to the sinking St Peter, with a simple inscription below, "Trust in the Lord." God's answer was clear, "If I am the Master of the Universe, am I not able to do what you might think impossible? If I can make a man walk on water, can I not help you succeed in this legal issue. Oh, man of little faith. All I ask is for you to place all your

TRUST in Me. HUMILITY DOES NOT MEAN SURRENDER." Immediately, Peter called his legal counsel and his message was brief, "Prepare for battle."

The Business Card Shows Up

Preparations were being made for battle and Polydeck was gathering all the documentation surrounding the research and development of their products. An exact timeline was being established for every move. This was critical in order to prove that their products had been developed independently, and that all of the research dates were prior to any work done by their competitor. In an effort to prove their respective positions, depositions were being conducted by both sides.

Then, out of the blue, Peter received a call from the CEO of the attacking company. "Peter, I would like to meet with you prior to my deposition." The following day Peter and the CEO met in a neutral location. Peter was prepared for the meeting and he had decided that this was not going to be a meeting of comparing documents and timelines. That would be done in court. This was not going to be a meeting to see what could be done to simply resolve the issue. This was the "line in the sand" meeting between David and Goliath, and Peter had only one weapon.

After the CEO stated his position, Peter calmly reached into his pocket and took out his business card, "You already know my name, and my position with the company, but I would like for you to read the back of our business card. I would like you to know who we are, what I stand for, and what our company stands for. I think this in only fair, so that you might know what you are up against. The CEO took the business card, read it, and held on to it. "These are good values."

Peter replied, "I want you to know that Honesty is the core value that our company stands by, and when I get deposed, and I am in front of that judge, I want you to know that I am going to speak the truth. In addition, I want you to know that in front of God, whether you acknowledge it or not, you have an equal responsibility to tell the truth of what your intentions are behind this whole thing."

The room was quiet. Peter had spoken what God had impressed on him; now the work was out of Peter's hands. The CEO was quiet for a long time. Slowly, but clearly, a change came over him. Not just a change of attitude, but a visible change. The CEO replied, "These values are good, and I would like to live by these same values. And with these values, I don't know that I can get in front of the judge and be deposed. I want to talk."

For the next hour and a half Peter and the CEO talked back and forth as gentlemen, truly looking for the right resolution. At the end of their time Peter asked, "Can we agree to certain conditions, to negotiate this thing and settle it?" The CEO's answer was simple: "Yes."

From there Peter and the CEO worked out a plan that simply described how all three suits would be resolved. The final point was that this resolution would be "with prejudice," meaning that it is in fact final, and that no further action would be taken. The document was signed by both parties, and everyone went home satisfied that a reasonable solution was possible.

The relief did not last long because on the following day Peter received a phone call from the attorneys representing the CEO's company. They called to inform Peter that they considered the document to be void, and of no value. The attorneys maintained that the wording of the document did not intend for it to be binding on both parties.

What had happened was really quite simple. During their meeting the day before, Peter had stated his Core Values, and the power of the Holy Spirit had taken control of the meeting, and of the men. Under the power of the Holy Spirit their objectives had been one—find the resolution that before God is true and right. The following day as the CEO and the company representatives met, the Holy Spirit was not present.

Now, there was only one path to take. Ultimately, the case would end up in court; thus the challenge for Goliath was that now Peter had his copy of the document that the CEO had signed, in which the issues were clearly defined and simply resolved. The day of court arrived and both sides stated their positions with great complexity. At the end of Polydeck's presentation the judge was given a copy of the agreement between Peter and the CEO.

After a close examination and review of the law, the judge declared the agreement as binding, and the case was dismissed, in favor of Polydeck.

The battle was over and David had faced Goliath, armed with one simple weapon, *Honesty*. Peter and Polydeck won the case. Peter was safe, Polydeck was safe, and the future of their employees was safe. A battle that no human could have hoped to win, against the Goliath of the industry, had been won by God's grace.

Peter was not naïve, for he realized that honesty was not always the deciding factor. He knew that when the Holy Spirit enters the room, many are so resistant to that gentle prodding that they will only be ruled by their own greedy self-interests. Peter's commitment to adhere to the Core Values, to answer first to God, must be complete. Sometimes that commitment would work out in his favor and sometimes, maybe not, but it would always work out in his favor with his relationship with God. If Peter believed that God owned his business, Honesty and Integrity were two values that the Owner was simply not ready to factor into the COB (Cost of Business).

Afterthought

This incident between David and Goliath took place several years ago, and Peter has not had the occasion to speak with the CEO since that time; however, he does often wonder. The CEO had seen and experienced the power of the Holy Spirit and more than that, he saw the Holy Spirit protect a man and a company that were governed by Christian Core Values. Where is this CEO today? Is it possible that this experience was a turning point in his life, as well as his business dealings? Is it possible that this example will be a turning point in your life or business?

Reflection

In the book of 1 Samuel, in chapter 17, the story was told of David and Goliath. There was an impending battle between the warring nations of Philistine and Israel. Each of the armies was encamped on a hillside, with a valley between them. Every morning for 40 days the nine and a half foot tall giant—Goliath—would come out from the Philistine camp and challenge the Israelites to send out one man to fight him, and to let the outcome between the two nations rest on the winner of this battle. The Israelites had never seen a man the size of Goliath or faced such a man in battle. The Philistine army was intimidating enough, but now they were faced with a giant.

At that same time there was a family from Bethlehem that was headed by a man named Jesse. Now, Jesse was the father of eight sons and advanced in years, and while he was too old to fight, three of his sons were in the army of Israel. Jesse's youngest son, David, had stayed behind to tend to the family herd, and to serve his brothers by taking food to the battle front.

One day while David was visiting his brothers, Goliath came out for his daily taunt. As usual, the men of Israel were scared to death at the mere sight of this giant, and withdrew as far as they could.

Upon seeing this giant, and hearing his taunt, David inquired of his brothers and the other soldiers as to what was happening. The soldiers were offended that the scrawny lad would be so bold as to ask about something having to do with battle. Finally, David's question fell on the ears of Saul, the commander of Israel's army. Saul, too, felt that David was a pitiable underdog to be in a battle.

David informed Saul that he intended to fight Goliath, and he was sure of a victory because Goliath and the Philistines had come up against "the armies of the living God." Then, David took a stick in his hand, along with five smooth stones and his sling, and went out to meet Goliath. As the giant taunted the youth, David replied, "You come to me with a sword, a spear, and a javelin, but I come to you in the name of the Lord of hosts, the God of the armies of Israel, whom you have taunted."

While today we might think it reckless of David to come up against such a giant, David did have a couple of things going for him that Goliath did not know about. First, being a Jew, David was aware of the Hebrew covenant with God, where God had promised that they would be a "great nation forever." Based on that, David knew that Israel would not be destroyed. I have to wonder, though, whether he really knew how that might happen. Although the nation of Israel would continue, was he completely confident that he would win his skirmish?

We have no way of knowing the mind of David,

but by his actions, he knew that he was on the right side, the side of God, and that he was prepared to face the giant, and depend on God for the outcome Facing giants was frightening. They may be bigger, more powerful, have more money, and they may not have a particularly high moral bar, but the God of David was a "giant-slayer." It was, after all, God's battle anyway.

Note:

The following is a copy of a note from the attorney representing Polydeck in the action described above. The note reflects the exponential effect of your testimony. This singular incident impacts the principals of the company that was at odds with Polydeck, the attorneys representing Polydeck, the Sunday School class members of this particular attorney, and any friends or clients with whom the attorney shares the story.

From the beginning of my representation of Polydeck, the card impressed upon me that Polydeck and its CEO were serious about their core beliefs in Christ, integrity, and ethics. Not only did Polydeck have an official statement of their values and beliefs, but the company rather unashamedly declared this statement on their business card. In my very first meeting with Polydeck's CEO to discuss a serious lawsuit that had been filed against the company, Peter's initial conversation with me was not what I would have expected. In a first meeting with the officers of a company served with a lawsuit in federal court, usually the conversation begins with questions about chances of success, the costs of the litigation, and my strategy. While the conversation eventually turned to these important topics, Peter began the conversation by explaining to me the seriousness of his faith, Polydeck's value system, and by providing me with a business card having the company's values printed on one side. It was immediately clear to me that the company's core beliefs were not relegated to a logo or motto, Polydeck was actually living and practicing its values and beliefs. This conclusion was reinforced repeatedly throughout our successful defense of the litigation.

Paul writes in Romans that he is not ashamed of the Gospel of Christ. Not long after my meeting with Peter, I provided the card to members of a Sunday School class that I teach as an example of someone who was not ashamed of his beliefs. I exhorted the class to never fear standing up for what they believe in.

—CHAPTER 9—

QUALITY YOU CAN COUNT ON?

With the momentum created by the Vegas encounter, Peter decided that it was time to share the Core Values statement with the entire Polydeck workforce. Many times Peter had been asked why so much time had elapsed between the "Silent Retreat" and the introduction of the Core Values. He related how it was a conscious decision to first *display* the Love of God in a real practical way before he *declared* God in the company. They wanted to make sure that people could see that this was an authentic statement backed by practical deeds of caring for their employees, families and community. Their words must be backed by real action—honesty and integrity—not some statement that could be viewed as hypocritical. Peter knew that if they were going to get buy-in from their multi-cultural, multi-faith staff, they had to "walk the walk" before they could "talk the talk."

When the Core Values were established there was a buzz throughout Polydeck. Everyone was excited about the changes, as well as the totally different environment at the "new" Polydeck. As another step in defining the culture at Polydeck, Peter decided to allow all the employees to express their support for the Mission Statement and Core Values. What a great idea! Involve everyone in promulgating the "Core Values." What better way to make sure everyone was on board and singing the same song!

It didn't take long to fashion a statement sheet with the company logo across the top and beautiful calligraphy around the outer perimeter. Boldly in the center were the words of the Mission Statement and the Core Values. Below that was the department name, followed by a line for each person in the department to sign indicating their support. A copy was made for each department, and the various supervisors were looking forward to their department meetings and the excitement that the statement sheets would bring.

Prior to sending out the sheets to be signed, Peter called all the employees together for a meeting, "It has been six months since I addressed you at our Thanksgiving luncheon. As promised, we have worked hard to show you that we are serious and committed about demonstrating that we really do care for you. Today is the next step in our journey to making this a great place to work. We have established a Core Value statement, which defines *how* we will operate this business and *why* we are in business. This statement is important to you as you now have a document by which you can hold me and the management team accountable to lead and conduct our business with Honesty, Integrity, Respect and Kindness. Should we fail at that, you have the right to challenge us at any time. My door is always open to you; however, I want you to know that with every right there comes a responsibility, and you will be responsible to conduct yourself according to these same values. As far as the religious component of the statement is concerned, the values in our statement are shared by many faiths, and I want you to know that we will respect all faith beliefs. To each faith we want to share Mother Teresa's sentiments by saying that our goal is to provide you with a loving and caring environment, and we encourage our Christians of any denomination to be the best Christian you can be. To our Muslims to be the best Muslim you can be, and to our Buddhists, to be the best Buddhist you can be. As a company, we will strive to Honor God in all we do, but we have placed the word "Strive" in there, because we are all human and we will fail at some point. But we want you and the world to know that we will continue to strive for this lofty goal. As I mentioned at the Thanksgiving lunch, the last statement reflects the importance of you as our employees, and the value that each of you contribute to our business. You are truly our greatest asset, and we intend to care for you that way."

It didn't take long for the statement sheets to make the rounds. Within a couple of days the department heads were back in Peter's office and anxious to show him the evidence of the complete support of the entire team, but it didn't work out quite that way. One by one, each department head gave his report, and one by one, the statement sheets were presented with the signature of every member of that department. At least until it came time for the molding department to report.

William, the department supervisor shared, "We had a great response. Everyone was excited to see what was happening and everyone thought it was a terrific idea to show their support by signing the sheet, that is, all but one."

Peter responded, "All but one! I hope you were clear with everyone that we are not asking everyone to state that they are Christians and that there was no pressure to sign. This is merely a statement of their support of the mission and values of the company. They do not necessarily, even have to agree with the source of those values."

"We were all abundantly clear. Everyone signed without a second thought, except Robert and his problem was not with the Christian aspect of the Core Values. He just said that he could not—in clear conscience—sign the sheet with the statements written the way they were."

"Please see if Robert is willing to meet with me. I really need to know what his resistance is and to make sure that we have not offended him in any way."

A short time later, Robert came to visit Peter in his office. "Robert, I truly hope we have not offended you in any way and I hope you understand that signing the sheet is completely voluntary. Would you mind sharing with me what you are thinking?"

"Mr. Freissle, I appreciate all the changes here, and I really appreciate both the Mission Statement and the Core Values, but I just could not sign that sheet with those statements about 'uncompromising quality standards', and 'honesty' and 'integrity'."

"What could you possibly mean? We manufacture one of the finest products in the industry."

"I know we do, Mr. Freissle, but quite honestly, with the tools that I have to work with, I can't honestly say that we are achieving 'uncompromising quality standards.' My tools are worn out."

Peter was floored. Robert was not resisting the signing because he disagreed with the statements. He was resisting because he did not believe that Polydeck lived up to the statements. Immediately, William was called back in the room and asked, "Is this true? Is it possible that we have this man working with tools that are so worn that they limit the quality of his work?" William responded, "Unfortunately, yes, it is not in the budget to replace the tools, and they are getting the job done, for the time being."

"William, I certainly appreciate the budget issues, but in clear conscience, I cannot ask one of our people to work under circumstances that would conflict with our very mission. You have my word that by the end of this week we will come up with a solution for this tool issue. They will be replaced."

The tools were quickly replaced. Peter realized that the Mission Statement and Core Values reach beyond Polydeck's customers. They reach to their own backyard. The Mission Statement and Core Values must impact every Polydeck stakeholder, employee, vendor, customer, and the surrounding community. If any stakeholder is left the opportunity to question the validity of the Mission Statement or the Core Values, it dilutes their worth in every area. The beginning of the Core Value statement is clear and broad in meaning: We are a company...

Oh! By the way, Robert signed the statement sheet.

———

The Operations Team meeting had been going

well, when the discussion turned to how they planned to implement the Mission Statement and Core Values in a practical way. Peter was taking a strong position that Polydeck needed to make sure that they strictly adhered to both, and that he was ready to face the cost and responsibility for both.

Mike finally chimed in, "Peter, I totally agree with everything on the business card, and I am in agreement that that is the way to do business. But, if we are going to put that card out there and if we are going to tell our employees that this is who we are and what we stand for, we have to ask ourselves a big question, 'Are we able to back it up, and are we able to back it up right now?'"

Peter replied, "What do you mean? Why wouldn't we be able to back it up? We can do whatever we want to."

"Peter, I'm sitting here with thousands of dollars of warranty claims on my desk. Standard procedure for us and for everyone else in the industry, as far as I know, is to pay as little on these warranty claims as possible. I have to be honest with you right now. When I look at these claims, I know that there is a difference in what we can get away with paying, and the 'right thing to do.' If we start paying these claims the way you are talking about, it will have a tremendous impact on the bottom line."

Mike was right; the impact would be tremendous. While Polydeck built a fine product and strict attention was given to quality control, there is a bit of leeway when manufacturing anything. Some number of warranty claims were simply a result of operating within that leeway.

"Mike, that's a good point, although a painful one. We still need to scrutinize all warranty claims. I am not advocating paying all claims without question, but I do believe that if we are going to operate with the integrity, we need to conduct the appropriate investigation. When there is a question, we need to give the customer the benefit of the doubt. Moving forward, we must pay any part of the claim where it is clear that Polydeck is at fault. In addition, any claim where the fault is unclear or where we recognize that Polydeck had a part in the failure, we need to pay the claim right away. It's the right thing to do."

Well, the Operations Team had been right. There was a tremendous impact on the bottom line. The warranty process became much easier, because they were not working as hard trying to avoid paying claims. The process was complicated even more, because it did not take long before the expectations from the customer were raised. Polydeck was doing the "right thing", but the "right thing" was costing them dearly. Something had to change. They simply could not afford to keep paying the warranty claims at that rate.

The answer was clear—the warranty claims were legitimate, so the only way to lower the warranty costs was to improve the quality of the product. An analysis was done of all facets of operations, from tooling to processes to product application, and the standard was reset for each step. The new standards were so stringent that in some cases it required new tools and equipment, even retraining of some of the sales team for product application and performance.

The initial cost of the warranty decision was difficult to handle. And the costs continued to come with retooling and training, but the decision had a terrific payoff. First, everyone associated with the process knew that he was manufacturing and selling a product that was one of the finest quality products in the industry. Second, eventually, warranty claims diminished to the point where they were negligible. Third, the improved quality and extra-knowledgeable sales team resulted in markedly increased sales. Customers worldwide know that when they purchase the Polydeck product, they were purchasing a product that was manufactured according to strict standards and that the installation and application was going to be right on target. In addition, these customers know that when they are dealing with Polydeck they have a relationship that is "performance guaranteed."

Reflection

It did not take Robert long to make the connection between "honesty", "integrity", and "uncompromising quality standards." Robert had been at Polydeck for a while, and it was easy for him, and others, to measure the quality of his work. When the standard changed from "get the job done" to actually being a standard of "uncompromising quality standards," things became complicated for Robert.

It did not take Mike long to envision the tremendous cost associated with making a promise that they were not yet equipped to stand behind.

God's Word applies the same basic standard to the work of all believers. Colossians 3:23–24 states, "Whatever you do, work at it with all your heart, as working for the Lord, not for human masters, since you know that you will receive an inheritance from the Lord as a reward. It is the Lord Christ you are serving."

Most of us are clear as to whom it is we report to on the job. Some of us report directly to a Board of Directors. Some employees report to an executive team, some to a manager, and others to a line leader. Regardless of our position in the workplace, the Bible is clear that ultimately, we report to Jesus Christ. Wouldn't it be interesting if Jesus Christ were in our next "team" meeting, regardless of the level of the team? How might that change things? How might it change both the interaction as well as the goals of the meeting?

If we are to be "working for the Lord" first, we must determine whether there is any redemptive value in our work. Surely, there is redemptive value in simply providing jobs and income for our employees, assuming that our business or industry is not engaged in practices that might be considered to be at odds with the will of Christ.

Redemptive value should not be construed to be so spiritually directed as to mean that the business must be ministry related. It might be as simple as providing building materials for homes, or providing chemicals that might improve the output of farms, thereby increasing food supplies. It might be as simple as providing a screen media for mines, allowing them to insure the quality of their materials produced, and lowering the cost of production of coal, salt, etc.

At one point Polydeck had to make some key decisions concerning growth. As a family business, did they really want or need to grow much larger? They had all they need, and with growth comes additional work and additional pressures. The answer came from one of the employees. When asked what he thought of the "new" Polydeck he remarked, "Over the years Polydeck has grown at a tremendous rate and what I really like about growth here is that as we grow we give more back to the community. We are able to make a positive impact on more people and bring to them a glimpse of God"

Once the redemptive value of our pursuit is determined, then we must examine our own personal position and product. If our work is truly "for the Lord", then we must examine both the quality of our work and the condition of our heart.

As economic stressors take their toll on both our business and personal finances, this often affects our attitude toward our workplace and co-workers. If we truly believe that "God is in control", then the mere fact that we are in that job means that for that season, we are where God would have us. And, if we are where God would have us, regardless of how difficult or uncomfortable it might be at the time then we must make sure that our "work product" is of the highest quality.

Your "work product" might be digging ditches. If it is, then you must make sure that you dig ditches as well as you possibly can, for you are digging ditches for the Lord. Your "work product" might be selling cars. Then you must sell cars as well as you can and with the highest integrity, for you are selling cards for the Lord. Your "work product" might be running a company with twenty thousand employees. Then you must make sure you operate that company with the highest integrity, treating both your employees and your customers as "neighbors," making all of your decisions as though your primary coach and counselor is Jesus Christ. For after all, "It is the Lord Christ you are serving."

— CHAPTER 10 —

THE GREAT
RECESSION

The Mission Statement and the Core Values were in place, and things have changed dramatically at Polydeck. From a company where employees could not wait to get out of the building, to a company where working conditions have surpassed every employees dreams. The Core Values were being lived out throughout the company. The leadership team was blessed by the new standards. They had the comfort and satisfaction of knowing that they were doing their work "as unto the Lord," and that they could be proud of everything that Polydeck did. The employees on the manufacturing floor had come to recognize their "new Polydeck" as a family that both cared for and about each other.

There was no evidence that any customers had hesitated to do business based on the Business Card. On the contrary, as customers came to realize that they were doing business with a company with integrity, the Polydeck reputation was growing. Business was good and the working environment was great. What could possibly go wrong?

It has been over two years since the inception of the Core Values and the adoption of the Business Card, but without warning, inexplicably, business dropped off by over twenty-five percent. Not just at Polydeck, but industry-wide.

This significant decline in revenue raises all sorts of questions. How did this happen? Why did this happen? The how and why are important, but the most important thing right now is "how do we respond and adjust to the tremendous drop in revenue?" There was no way Polydeck could survive a revenue drop such as this without cutting payroll expense; basically, this meant laying people off.

For over two years Peter and the Polydeck leadership team had been working to convince the entire company that Polydeck was going to operate as a "family." The leadership team viewed all of the employees at every level of the operation as "neighbors", and Peter and the leadership team had to come up with the best business solution possible, while still honoring their "family" and neighbors.

In February of 2009, Polydeck held their monthly "Birthday and Anniversary" meeting. In this meeting all birthdays and anniversaries are acknowledged, as well as awards and rewards given out.

Immediately following all of the opening announcements, Peter stepped to the front of the room. The first thing he did was to invite those that would like to pray with him to "bow their heads", "Dear Heavenly Father we humbly come before you to thank you for the many blessings you have bestowed on our company. We have enjoyed growth and success, but now we are faced with a serious recession. Help us to remember the events depicted in the stained glass window in our chapel, in which your disciples were caught in the middle of a storm in their small boat, and how Jesus seemed to be asleep and not to care and how easily He was able to calm the storm. Help us to remember His words, "'Why are you frightened? Have you no Faith?' It is with faith in you that we come before you to ask you to lead us through this storm. Amen."

The next thing Peter did was present a poster with a graph of revenue for the past few years, and he compared it to the twenty-five percent drop that had persisted for the last three months. The drop in revenue was dramatic. Peter explained that there were only a couple of options to reduce costs enough to protect the company. Many of Polydeck's competitors had laid off employees, with additional reductions to come and for Polydeck to do what was necessary would require laying off one of every five employees.

The Polydeck leadership team did not think that that was the right thing to do, and they believed that (hoped that, prayed that), as a family, there might be a better solution. In addition, they agreed that changes needed to be made incrementally, determined by the economic impact. The first step would require hourly cuts and payroll cuts. These cuts would extend to employees at every level, hourly and salaried. They would share the pain together.

There! He had said it. There would be pay cuts, as well as time reductions. This was the best way to care for their "family." Peter held his breath waiting for the response. It finally came. It began with just a few scattered around the room. They began to clap. Within moments, everyone was clapping. Within moments of that, many began to stand and clap in appreciation for the decisions of their leadership.

Trust is a powerful binding agent and it was clear that the "family" knew that the leadership team would make decisions that were in both the best interest of the company as well as in the best interest of the members of the "family." As overwhelmed as Peter was with the standing ovation, they still had to get through the Birthday and Anniversary meeting. Different employees were recognized, and everyone clapped in congratulations.

Awards were given out during the final part of the meeting. Over time, different awards had been established as a token of appreciation from the company. The recognition was as important as the award, but a cash award is always appreciated. That month there was a Production Award for reaching certain production goals and the award went to a gentleman named William. Surrounded by applause, William made his way to the front of the room and he was presented with an award check for fifty dollars. The fifty dollars would pay for a nice dinner for William and his wife.

Without hesitation William received his check, and without hesitation, William turned to Peter and gave him the check back, "Now is not a good time for this. Let's leave this in for now. Maybe I can collect it later, when things are better."

Sometimes, families are a bit odd. Sometimes it is the uncle or cousin that hardly says a thing, but when they finally speak, it is profound. William's actions spoke volumes to Peter. The love and trust that Peter had worked so hard to instill had just come back to him, but William's actions had spoken equally as loud to the other Polydeck employees.

Immediately following the meeting, Peter stepped into the restroom to wash his face and collect himself. The next surprise came when he exited the restroom. The lights were off in the hall. Surely they were not having electrical problems on top of everything else. No. No electrical problems. Already the employees had taken it upon themselves to find any way possible to cut expenses, and they had begun by turning off any unnecessary lights.

Reflection

In retrospect, there is no question that the Polydeck leadership team made the right decision in adjusting hours and pay. Within two quarters the environment within the industry had changed and sales, as well as revenues, had started on the road to recovery. Employee hours and pay were adjusted back to the pre-crash levels. Since that time sales have continued to grow and this growth has been reflected in employee pay and benefits.

Let's be realistic. There were no guarantees that the recovery would occur within a couple of quarters. There were no guarantees that down-sizing would not be required eventually, but the story was not in the specific decision to reduce hours and pay. The story was in the trust expressed by the employees.

Trust is not the result of holding the position of CEO. Trust is not a by-product of being the owner or boss. Trust is earned over time. Trust is a commodity that separates the companies for which we want to work, from the companies that merely provide jobs. Trust is something that exists in "families", not with mere "employers."

In Acts 5: 1-11 we are told the story of Ananias and his wife, Sapphira. In Chapter 4 we are told that the members of the early church were voluntarily sharing their possessions in an effort to care for those in need. Ananias and Sapphira sold a piece of property for the same purpose, yet when they were questioned as to the selling price they were less than forthcoming (they lied). The Scripture explains that in lying, they lied not only to man, but they had lied to God. The punishment for their lie was absolute. They both fell dead.

Now let's be perfectly clear. Polydeck, or your business, is not the church. Yet there is no reason that your business should not be run with the same principles as the church. The words of Ananias and Sapphira could not be trusted, and the result was that they died.

We all understand that there must be a certain degree of confidentiality when running any business. A competitive environment prevents complete disclosure. It is sound business practice and common sense that our finances and business practices are not openly shared with everyone.

This is addressed in Scripture. While it had been unsold, the property in question had been under the control of Ananias and Sapphira and after it was sold it was up to them as to how to use the funds. They were not required to give the entire sale price to the church. Their sin was in lying about the sale price. Their sin was in knowing one thing, and saying something to the contrary. Their sin was in not being individuals of integrity.

The Scripture made a profound distinction when commenting on this sin. "Why is it that you have conceived this deed in your heart?" The words of Ananias and Sapphira were a reflection of what was in their hearts. That is where integrity begins, and that is where it must reside. When your employees know your heart and trust it, they will applaud your decisions.

PART 2
— CHAPTER 11 —

CARING IN THE WORKPLACE

As Peter gained new insight into the concept of treating his employees as "neighbors", he knew that he must make additional changes in the working conditions at Polydeck. The company already offered an Employee Assistance Program (EAP) and that did an adequate job of providing some telephone based resources for the employees, but Peter wanted to provide something more tangible. Peter wanted to provide something that might help meet the spiritual needs of the employees, without being offensive, or being misconstrued as pushing his beliefs on his workforce.

After meeting with a friend of his and sharing his thoughts, Peter came up with the perfect solution: Corporate Chaplains of America. Corporate Chaplains of America (CCA) is a non-denominational ministry that provides care to employees for personal and professional life issues. While Peter was not intimately familiar with CCA, a reading of their mission statement convinced him that this was exactly what he needed.

"Our mission is to build caring relationships with the hope of gaining permission to share the life changing Good News of Jesus Christ in a non-threatening manner."

Peter had experienced a life-changing awakening at the "silent retreat" but in order to continue to grow and stay on the "right path", Peter was receiving regular spiritual guidance from his pastor. Peter realized the importance of this spiritual support and desperately wanted to meet the spiritual needs of his employees, but as a businessman he was intimately aware of the risks involved in bringing in a chaplaincy ministry. A brief conversation with CCA convinced him that this ministry was acutely aware of the boundary issues and that the CCA chaplains were well-trained and diligent to respect these boundaries with people of all faiths.

All of the CCA chaplains have a workplace background, as well as seminary or Bible-college training which ensures that the chaplain can relate to the issues that the employees must deal with. In addition, upon joining CCA, each chaplain goes through an extensive training program that ensures their proficiency in areas such as counseling, hospital visitation, dealing with substance abuse issues, and dealing with marital issues.

Corporate Chaplains of America was a tremendous addition to the Polydeck culture. It was made clear when the chaplain was introduced that any interaction between the employees and the chaplain was strictly at the discretion of the employee. In addition, any conversation between the chaplain and the employees was confidential. The chaplain was being provided as a ministry to the employees and confidentiality was essential.

The CCA chaplain visits their facility weekly and has total access to everyone in the company. Strict attention is given to not interfering with workflow, but the chaplain makes sure that everyone knows when he will be around. Over time, the chaplain develops a relationship of trust with the employees and it is this trust relationship that allows employees to share their personal needs with the chaplain.

Since first joining Polydeck, the CCA chaplain has counseled with dozens, if not hundreds, of families. He has played a major role in helping individuals conquer substance abuse issues and has visited many employees and employee family members when they were hospitalized.

All of these ministry opportunities have been important, but most importantly, since CCA began ministering at Polydeck, as of this writing, there have been sixty-three professions of faith in Jesus Christ. And, the chaplain doesn't leave it there. Whenever an employee accepts Jesus Christ as their Savior, with the permission of the employee, the CCA chaplain mentors that employee through a discipleship program that familiarizes them with both the Old and the New Testament, grounds them in the "fundamentals of the faith", and helps the new believer find a church where they will be both spiritually fed and comfortable.

Although Polydeck's chaplain works for Corporate Chaplains of America, he has become an integral part of the Polydeck family. Not only does the chaplain make his weekly "rounds", and his hospital visits and counseling sessions, you will find him at the cookouts and ballgames as well. Peter has found that this "first step" in providing care for his employees had become such a valuable addition to the family, the fact that they provide a Corporate Chaplain has become a drawing card for new employees.

"The Corporate Chaplain system is something great. I had never heard of it before I came to Polydeck, and we started it up since I've come to work here. Jeff is unbelievable as our Corporate Chaplain. What astounded me was within a couple of weeks of his coming here he could name anybody by name in the whole plant. He just became a part of us."

On a personal point, my sister was sick and on life support machines, and we were going to unplug the machines. My pastor was out of town at the time, out of state actually. Jim called Jeff (Corporate Chaplain), and he was at the hospital about before I was. He was with us, and he was praying with us, my family and I, as my sister passed away. So, I'm uh, really up on the Corporate Chaplains." - Phil, a Polydeck employee.

— CHAPTER 12 —

CARING
COMMITTEE

———————

With the tremendous changes in the attitudes and management style at Polydeck, plus the integration of Corporate Chaplains of America, the cultural change at Polydeck was palpable. Everyone at Polydeck could both see and feel the effects of this "spiritual awakening" and the concepts of "family" and "neighbors" were quickly becoming the everyday norm. The attitude of the leaders had changed so significantly that production had actually increased now that people were working where the "Son" shone, instead of under a cloud of intimidation and stress.

Everything was moving along well. In a matter of months Polydeck had transformed into a place where people looked forward to going to work, but something was still missing. Peter's relationship with Christ and with his leadership team was growing. The leadership team itself was developing spiritually, and thoroughly enjoying the benefits of growing together; however, while the manufacturing workforce enjoyed the benefits of a great workplace and the great ministry of Corporate Chaplains of America, they didn't have their own vehicle for "living out their faith," and developing their workplace relationships into "neighbors."

This need to involve everyone in the "neighborhood" resulted in the formation of the Caring Committee. Initially the Caring Committee was established as a way of reaching out to the community and allowing Polydeck employees to help in home repairs for outside families in need, but eventually one of the Polydeck employees came forward and pointed out that the Core Values states that the greatest asset was the Polydeck employees themselves. Why not set the committee up so that they can provide both "in reach" as well as "outreach" for the Polydeck employees.

[As Polydeck employees became more involved in the "community," the idea and attitude continued to grow. At the time of this writing the Caring Committee oversees eight different funds. Senior management determines the total annual Caring Committee budget, currently a percentage of gross revenue, and the Caring Committee determines how much is allocated to each fund.]

Benevolent Fund

While the rest of the funds are funded completely from the Caring Committee budget, the Benevolent Fund is a bit different. When a request comes to the Caring Committee this request is thoroughly reviewed by the Committee, and then put to a vote. Once the Caring Committee determines that the request is a worthy cause, each member of the Caring Committee then solicits donations from their individual departments. Employees in each department have an opportunity to donate for each individual need. The Caring Committee then matches these funds at a ratio of four dollars for every one dollar donated.

Recently, the fund was expanded to include fundraising events that fellow employees arrange for an employee in need. A recent example was when an event was arranged to fund the medical expenses of a rare disease of an employee's daughter that caused significant burden on the employee due to extraordinary "out of pocket" expenses.

While this process is often humbling to the person in need, it provides every Polydeck employee the opportunity to have a tangible impact on their "neighbors." *The company surrounded me at a time of difficulty helping me with my daughter that has osteoscarcoma, which is bone cancer. The Caring Committee presented an envelope to all the employees in the plant, and everybody pitched in, and it came out to be almost two thousand dollars." - Jerry, a Polydeck employee.*

Community Charity Fund

You may recall in an earlier chapter the story of Peter being called out of a meeting, only to be confronted by the local sheriff's department, informing him that he was being sued. It was in this meeting that Peter was listening to a representative from Campus Crusade sharing how he came to know Christ while in college, and explaining the tremendous impact that Campus Crusade had on his life, and on the lives of thousands of other students around the world. This humble speaker was convincing that any donation at all would yield great returns for "the kingdom."

The Community Charity Fund was established in 2007 as a way of living out the "social responsibility" mandate of the "Core Values." The Caring Committee has a list of over fifty local non-profit agencies. This list is compiled by asking every employee to submit three non-profit agencies of their choosing on an annual survey form. These agencies range from the homeless shelter and the Shiners' Hospital to cancer research and the local Christian radio station. On a rotating basis, each month, a ministry from this list will meet with the Caring Committee. At that time the ministry has the opportunity to present their program and explain to the Caring Committee how they would utilize any financial assistance provided. The Caring Committee then prayerfully makes a determination as to the level of assistance provided.

"We have had several charities come in, and they have all been so wonderful. This whole program has just influenced my heart so much. It has made me a better person." - a Polydeck employee.

"I've worked with some projects brought up by Caring Committee like United Way and Christmas in Action, and it's really brought a lot of pride in my own life, and fulfillment knowing that I'm helping those that are in need, and are less fortunate. And it's also brought employees closer together by working together outside the company" - Daniel, a Polydeck employee

Employee Home Repair Fund

This is a true in-reach program that helps Polydeck employees with homes that they own or occupy. It is one of the programs that bring the most personal satisfaction to the employees involved. There is a financial cap on Polydeck participation; however, the employee may pay for any repairs that exceed that cap. Fellow Polydeck employees volunteer their time, and the company provides the materials. Special attention is given to safety, health, and security issues such as smoke alarms, hot water and plumbing, heating and air, and electrical. If some of the repairs requested require expertise not available from the volunteers an outside firm may be brought in to help.

Employee Emergency Loan Fund

All Emergency Loan requests are kept confidential. There is a financial cap on the loan amount, and the loans are repaid through payroll deduction. Employees may qualify for a loan every two years, but the previous loan must be paid in full before applying for a new loan.

The Employee Emergency Loan may be used to supplement the Employee Home Repair Fund. Special attention is given to home repairs, transportation, utilities, and safety and health needs.

Reach Out Fund

The Reach-Out Fund is to provide funding for mission related projects and marriage conferences. These mission-related projects may be as simple as participating in the local March of Dimes walks, or as great as helping fund a Polydeck employee in a foreign mission trip with their church.

With the close and confidential relationship that the Corporate Chaplain has developed over time, several employees are willing to discuss difficulties they are experiencing in their marriages. And, with the guidance and support of the Chaplain, a couple is encouraged to attend a marriage retreat that is suitable for their individual situation. This is where the "Reach out Fund" comes into play by providing the funds to send the couple on an "all expenses paid" weekend to remember. With approval from the Caring Committee, on a very limited basis, it is possible for a Polydeck employee to work on a local project while on company paid time. In this case, the employee's time is charged back to the Caring Committee budget.

Employee Car Repair Fund

The Emergency Car Repair Fund has turned out to be a life-saver for many of Polydeck employees. The challenge with car troubles is that we are never ready for them when they come. The Emergency Car Repair Fund is strictly for emergency repairs. It may not be used for maintenance, and it must be for the vehicle used by the employee or their spouse. There is a cap on the amount funded, as well as a yearly cap per employee. Each repair request is reviewed by the Caring Committee for approval.

Medical Emergency Fund

While Polydeck offers an excellent insurance program, sometimes employees have a difficult time meeting the co-pay or the deductible. In this case, the Medical Emergency Fund steps up to stand in the gap. As with the other funds, there is an annual cap on this fund, however in this case, the need is limited by the insurance coverage.

General Fund

Each year some revenue is set aside to fund projects that are used to improve the workplace, or to benefit the general welfare of the employees. For instance, the General Fund has helped fund work boots and gloves, given out Wal-Mart Gas card, Ingles Grocery cards, and funded a family picnic and day of rides at an amusement park for all employees and their family members.

Caring Committee Guidelines

Each department is represented on the Caring Committee, and members serve for a period of one year. The only positions that do not rotate off are two representatives from senior management and the Human Resources facilitator. There are a few issues that are considered out-of-bounds for the Caring Committee. Issues having to do with pay rates, pay scales, employee benefits, or criticism of a particular employee are absolutely not discussed. The purpose of the Caring Committee is to create and administer programs for the welfare of the employees and their families, the work environment, and the community. *And I think this Caring Committee has united the whole company together. Now we*

are like one whole family. It doesn't matter whether we are white, black, Asian, Hispanic. It doesn't matter. We are a family. And anytime someone needs somebody, we are going to jump on it. We are going to be there for them"
- Pam, a Polydeck employee.

−CHAPTER 13−

I CAUGHT
YOU CARING

One of the most successful and most treasured programs at Polydeck is "I Caught You Caring." As the Caring Committee worked through how Polydeck could celebrate the Core Values detailed on the back of the business card, it occurred to them that special attention should be given to specific examples of living out the Core Values. So often companies have "Core Values" but they are seldom turned into Real Life Action. The Caring Committee wanted to breathe life into the Core Values and celebrate and reward positive actions that supported our Christian values; thus the birth of "I Caught You Caring."

Employees could nominate fellow employees when they witnessed acts of honesty, integrity, positive attitude, kindness, compassion, or respect. The individuals nominated would receive special recognition at the monthly Birthday and Anniversary meeting. The leadership team and the Caring Committee were excited about this opportunity to celebrate their "neighbors." Special t-shirts were ordered with a big heart with "I Caught You Caring" across the front. This was going to be big!

Interestingly enough, the concept just could not get off the ground. Employees were given nomination sheets, and encouraged to nominate someone when they saw some specific example of the Core Values being lived out, but this was early in the game for the "new" Polydeck, and employees were skeptical as to how long it would last, or how it would be received. Human nature dictates that it seems so easy to stand around and talk about people's shortcomings and weaknesses, but to stand up and congratulate someone, even to celebrate with someone just doesn't come naturally.

Several months had passed and still there were no nominations. Finally the Caring Committee checked the nomination box, and there was one lonely slip of paper.

One of the janitors at Polydeck had recently been a bit down on his luck and was having personal, as well as financial challenges. Out of the blue, one of the lead men, Big Joe, called him up and told him that he was going to help him––financially. Unbeknownst to Big Joe, the janitor filled out the form and nominated Joe for "I Caught You Caring."

That month at the regular Birthday and Anniversary meeting the time had finally arrived. "We have another announcement today. Big Joe, would you please come forward. We would like to give you this month's award for "I Caught You Caring." Big Joe was astounded, surprised, but also proud. He had not intended that anyone would know of his kindness. What he had done was strictly between him and the janitor. On the other hand, Big Joe was honored that his kindness would be recognized and rewarded.

There was one problem though. THEY DIDN'T HAVE A T-SHIRT BIG ENOUGH TO FIT HIM!!! The Caring Committee considered this a good problem to have. It was a bit late, but Big Joe got his XXXL shirt.

The following month the "I Caught You Caring" box was full of nominations where employees had caught each other caring. Employees now thought differently about this program now that one of the most respected and strongest employees had served as an example. Now Polydeck employees can be identified throughout the Spartanburg community as they wear their special "I Caught You Caring" t-shirts. What a privilege it is for them when they are asked, "What's the deal with that shirt?"

"Monthly we meet and give a small gift to those that we have caught caring. It doesn't have to be a whole lot. Somebody gives somebody a lift home. Somebody helps somebody change a flat. Somebody's car won't start and they help them, or they lock their keys in their car. People

that find money just lying on the floor; a lot of times people would just stick it in their pocket, but the Caught You Caring and the Caring Committee has brought out something where it helps everyone of us care for our fellow employees. And, I like to think of us as a big family here at Polydeck" - Phil, a Polydeck employee.

–Chapter 14–

His Way
At Work

In 2007, as Peter's flight crossed the Pacific Ocean, the overflow of what God was doing in his life spilled onto the CEO seated next to him. Peter shared his business card and explained how God had transformed the why and how of his business. Testimony after testimony from Peter brought a consistent response from the hotel executive: "You can't do that and run a successful business!" Peter knew differently, but the question became...how could he help this leader and others like him break through these perceived barriers?

From the conversation on that flight there was a prompting in Peter's heart, combined with a sense that God had given him and Polydeck a gift. This was a gift that was not to be kept to themselves. Peter was stirred by Jesus' calling for believers to be salt and light...to not hide their light under a bowl, but to put it on a stand so it gives light to others. His prayers over the next couple of months sought guidance on how to share God's gift of love and care with other business leaders.

While the 2008 New Year rang in, Peter continued to sense God's calling to help others on a similar journey as his, but the question remained...how? To help with that question, he set up a lunch meeting with a friend—Scott Gajewsky. Peter first met Scott during a presentation to recruit Peter's church to get involved in the start-up of a ministry to help homeless families. On that October evening in 2004, Scott not only got support from the church to launch the ministry but a partnership began between Scott and Peter. A partnership grounded in a shared growing relationship with Christ and a responding motivation to help God's people in need. Over the next four years, they worked closely together on the homeless family ministry, and during side conversations Peter shared with Scott what God was doing at Polydeck. In 2005, during a similar "parking lot conversation" Scott recommended the services of Corporate Chaplains of America to Peter.

Listening to Peter share his heart and vision over lunch that January day in 2008, Scott was struck with the realization of how God had amazingly been preparing him for "such a time as this." Over the past nine years, God had been blending Scott's twenty-six years of business leadership experiences with his growing personal relationship with Christ and a passion to live out his faith in all areas of his life.

This blending of his work-life with ministry came to life for Scott in 1999 during several significant challenges in his early leadership role as Division Director of a printing plant in St. Petersburg Florida. An accidental death of an employee at Scott's plant brought him abruptly to the realization that he was not equipped to face this tragedy. As Scott drove to meet Buddy's family at the hospital, he cried out, "Father, help me, I do not know what to do." God answered in an inaudible whisper, "Focus on My people." A personal relationship with God came to life for Scott that day as reliance on his self was found empty, and he experienced the mighty hand of his Lord now guiding his way. During the tragedy of Buddy's death, God revealed a new mission field to Scott—his workplace. God was calling him to "focus on all of his people", not just his wife and daughters, but his employees and their families as well.

During the second half of 1999, pressures to meet plant performance expectations mounted. Scott faced a new potential death experience, the death of his job. He knew his team could improve but he was not confident in his leadership style to help get them there. In desperation, he was tempted to try the "dictator" leadership style of…set goals then scream, threaten, fire and rehire if the goals are not meet. It was not the style that proved successful for him in the past, but time was running out. On the verge of a nervous breakdown and once again coming to the end of himself and his abilities,

Scott sought God's help. God answered this time through a book. During a trip back to Tampa after a "rough" meeting at the corporate office in Chicago, Scott grabbed a new release at an airport bookstore entitled, *Leadership by the Book*. He recognized the authors, Ken Blanchard, Bill Hybels, and Phil Hodges, but it was not until after take-off that Scott realized "the Book" was the Bible. As he read on, the Servant Leader model of Jesus came to life for the first time. Scott's previously compartmentalized "religion" was now being transformed into a 24/7 relationship with his Lord and Savior Jesus Christ. Guided by his Servant Leader coach, Jesus, he successfully led the plant's performance turnaround in his new mission field, his workplace.

Scott's mind returned to his lunch conversation with Peter and the questions at hand,

• How do we help other Christian business leaders love God and love God's people in their workplace by creating an environment where Christian values and virtues are truly lived out?

• How do we help folks take what they learn on Sundays at Church (or through books or seminars) and apply it to how they live Monday through Saturday?

• How do we help people in the workplace display the love of Christ and declare Jesus as the source of that love in a non-threatening manner?

• How do we help leaders navigate the "fears" associated with making these God glorifying changes in their workplace?

• How do you help leaders develop and implement a "Ministry Plan" or "Caring Plan" for their organization?

• How do we utilize all the excellent workplace ministry tools already available by helping get them in the hands of folks who are seeking to change?

• How do we help knock down implementation barriers, including costs, by offering coaching services for no required fee?

Over the next three months, with much prayer and guidance from Godly leaders in the workplace ministry movement, the non-profit ministry, "His Way At Work" was birthed to try and address all those questions/opportunities listed above. It was officially launched on March 31, 2008 with Scott serving as its Executive Director & Workplace

Ministry Coach.

The "His Way At Work" mission is: *To equip and encourage businesses to gradually transform into Christ-centered organizations that:*

- Operate on virtue based principles;

- Demonstrate authentic Christian caring, enabling them through the Holy Spirit to lead others to Christ.

During its first three years, "His Way at Work" has shared what God is doing in the workplace and how you can join His work to create eternal Kingdom value. These "seed casting" presentations have been made to many Christian business organizations, Church groups, Pastors, Community leader groups, private schools, public schools and universities in the U.S. and Mexico. Outside of these presentations, Scott has "coached" over 35 different organizations representing over 20,000 employees in five different countries.

For more information on "His Way At Work", please see *www.hiswayatwork.com* and *"The Business Card"* companion handbook.

—CHAPTER 15—

A FUTURE OF CARING

A Word From Peter

As I have contemplated the words of St. Francis of Assisi, "All the darkness in the world can't extinguish the light from a single candle." I hope that what follows is seen as my humble effort to shine my single candle in the hope that it may be useful to someone, even if it is small and imperfect.

Let me start by saying that as I begin to write this chapter I am painfully aware of my personal weaknesses and failings, and feel unworthy. After all, who am I with all my faults and failings to tell others what to do; however, after much prayer and counsel from godly advisors, I have come to realize that the events and experience of my life are a gift from God that has helped to transform my way of thinking and these gifts should be shared with others for their encouragement and for God's glory. So in a spirit of service rather than superiority, I present what God has done and revealed to me, in the hope that you may see His guiding hand in my life and that you may hear the same loving voice that whispered my name and said "Come follow me." With this in mind I offer you the story of my journey, filled with the same struggles and challenges each of us face and to assure you that you are not alone on this journey.

The challenge came to me as I began my "silent retreat", also known as "Spiritual Exercises." This is a program developed in the 16th century by Ignatius of Loyola, a Spanish Knight who founded the Jesuit monastic order. Within the first hour of my "silent retreat" I was confronted with a few tough questions:

• Do you truly believe in God?

• Do you believe in Eternity?

• If so, do you have a plan for your life that will lead you to spend Eternity with God?

• Is God the center of your life and do you allow Him to influence all the key decisions you make?

• Do you make regular time for God, where you escape from the "noise" of this world and in the silence of your heart seek to hear God's will and plan for your life?

• Have you compartmentalized your life in such a way as to exclude God from certain rooms in the house of your soul?

• Are you prepared to soften your heart and let God enter the house of your soul, and together with Him, inspect every room of it and allow Him unconditional access to "spring clean" those rooms that you have kept locked? Rooms where you have been hoarding your "junk."

As you can imagine, the "Silent Retreat" turned into a "Not so Silent Retreat", as I began the most intense and intimate dialogue that I had ever had with God. As our dialogue intensified I realized that "The Master of the Universe" truly loved me unconditionally. As I opened the doors to the rooms of my soul, I could feel the warmth of His love as He did some "spring cleaning" in each room. It was then that I heard Him whisper, "Your Sins are forgiven." It felt as though I had been through a "car wash" for my soul, and the joy and gratitude I felt was indescribable. I realized that even though I was a tiny speck on the face of the earth, God was interested in and wanted to be part of every tiny detail of my life. Wow! The Master of the Universe really did care about someone as insignificant as me, and he had a plan for my life.

As I spent the next two days pondering God's Plan for my life, I came to grips with a few very key issues:

• The first issue had to do with me and the way I viewed my accomplishments. The Root sin that was covering my eyes was pride and this pride of mine had given me the false perception that everything I had and all my achievements were MINE. I thought it was all about ME. It dawned on me that the success of the business was in fact not mine either, but rather as a result of the application of the business talents that God had given me.

• The second issue was similar, but dealt with the source of my possessions. Once I lifted the 'glasses of pride" through which I had viewed my world, I realized that all the things I treasured were in fact gifts from God. My wife, my family, my treasures, and my business. I remembered the parable of the servants to whom talents were given and after a while the master returned and asked the servants to give account of how they had used their talents. I had heard this parable so many times but suddenly it took on a whole new meaning for me. I was not the owner. I was merely a custodian/steward. God created it all and therefore owns it all.

• The final revelation came as I pondered Jesus' instructions to "Love your neighbors as yourself." My neighbors were all around me…my wife, family, employees, suppliers, competitors, everyone. To love my neighbor as myself means to love each of these that God has placed in my path.

My Silent Retreat was only the beginning of my walk toward God's will. The removal of the "glasses of pride" revealed that there was much work to do in every area of my life, and opened my eyes to the mission opportunity that God had given me.

My Mission

We began writing this book, excited about sharing a few of the many miracles that God has performed through our simple Core Values and our Business Card. I would like to close by sharing a mission that God has put on my heart.

As you have just read throughout the book, God has led me to completely change the way we do business at Polydeck. I know first-hand that choosing to completely change your way of doing business and the way you relate to employees, vendors, and customers, is not always going to be an easy decision. The changes here at Polydeck have taken place over a number of years and they continue. We have had missteps and stumbles. We have received tremendous counsel from many sources. It has been difficult at times, but the rewards we have received have been far greater than the risk or the effort.

Throughout the book, Steve shared a brief description of several of our ministries to our employees, but God has given us another ministry to which we are fully devoted. We hope to share our vision and our efforts with every business for which God will open the door. Implementing these changes (sometimes radical) can be difficult and seem as though you are on shaky ground. We want to partner with you in discovering what God can do in your life and in the life of your business when you truly make God the "Chairman of the Board."

To that end we are developing a companion handbook that will soon be released. Our prayer is that this handbook will be a tremendous tool, to help you better understand the power and the process of running your business in a manner that pleases Jesus Christ.

In Part One of this handbook we will share what we believe to be the reasons to implement these changes, as well as some considerations for not changing. We will discuss in detail the Barriers to Implementation, including the possible impact on every stakeholder. I will share with you some thoughts on your own spiritual journey, as you face this possibly unsettling task. Finally, I will share what we have found to be both tangible as well as spiritual benefits of doing business God's way.

Part Two will take you, step-by-step, through the process of identifying change areas for your specific workplace. We will help you formulate a strategic plan for implementation, and even help you build a timeline for your transition.

Why a handbook? As we look at what God has done in us and for us over these past few years, we believe that this book and the handbook are merely steps in our transition. We are striving to be obedient, and what better way to seek obedience than to share God's love with you, our neighbors.

Finally, we have told you that we want to partner with you. "His Way at Work" was formed with the singular mission of providing help and guidance to you. We believe that as we "walk this road" together we will be blessed beyond measure by God allowing us to have a small part in seeing the marketplace become His marketplace. Please contact "His Way at Work" at your earliest convenience to see how we might be able to serve you. In the meantime, thank you for allowing us to share our story. May God richly bless you, your family, and your ministry.

For a small taste of what you will find in the Companion Handbook, please take a few minutes to complete the Self Assessment and check out the listing of Potential Ministry (Caring) Activities found in Appendix A of this book.

Self Assessment & Potential Ministry (Caring) Plan Activities

Self Assessment

Leader's Personal Beliefs	Always 5	Often 4	Sometimes 3	Seldom 2	Never 1
I believe in and accept Jesus Christ as my Lord and Savior.	☐	☐	☐	☐	☐
I love God with all my heart, soul and mind.	☐	☐	☐	☐	☐
I love my neighbor as myself.	☐	☐	☐	☐	☐
I pray daily and seek God's wisdom and direction in all that I do.	☐	☐	☐	☐	☐
I encourage others to develop a personal relationship with God and I help disciple those seeking to grow in their faith.	☐	☐	☐	☐	☐

Leader's Business Beliefs	Always 5	Often 4	Sometimes 3	Seldom 2	Never 1
I believe God owns my company, which I am just a servant and a steward of what He has entrusted to me.	☐	☐	☐	☐	☐
I am committed to running my business on Biblical principles.	☐	☐	☐	☐	☐
I want the company to be inclusive of others and faith-friendly.	☐	☐	☐	☐	☐

Leader's Business Beliefs	Always 5	Often 4	Sometimes 3	Seldom 2	Never 1
I strive to operate the company with excellence to glorify God and profitably to fund the ministry of the company.	☐	☐	☐	☐	☐
I operate the business in ethical ways and with integrity.	☐	☐	☐	☐	☐

Leader's Style and Tone	Always 5	Often 4	Sometimes 3	Seldom 2	Never 1
My words and actions reflect to everyone my desire to conduct business according to Christian values and principles.	☐	☐	☐	☐	☐
I ensure that all employees know I am accessible through my "Open Door Policy".	☐	☐	☐	☐	☐
I display Christ's Love through my actions, showing appreciation and respect for all my employees and business contacts.	☐	☐	☐	☐	☐
I reflect a "servant leader" style of leadership as modeled by Jesus.	☐	☐	☐	☐	☐
I lead voluntary prayer during meetings and events.	☐	☐	☐	☐	☐

Organization's Strategy, Structure and Core Values	Always 5	Often 4	Sometimes 3	Seldom 2	Never 1
The business is performed with excellence in all areas and is used as a platform for ministry with our "bottom line profit" seen as a gift from God to be used to create Eternal Value.	☐	☐	☐	☐	☐
A Mission Statement is in place stating "what" the organization desires to accomplish.	☐	☐	☐	☐	☐
A Core Values Statement, grounded on Biblical principles, has been developed stating the "how" and "why" of the organization's actions.	☐	☐	☐	☐	☐
The Core Values Statement is available to all employees and ALL employees are held accountable to these values.	☐	☐	☐	☐	☐
The Core Values of the company are "lived out" through a strategic Ministry (Caring) Plan.	☐	☐	☐	☐	☐

Organization's Ministry (Caring) Strategy	Always 5	Often 4	Sometimes 3	Seldom 2	Never 1
The Ministry (Caring) Plan is incorporated into the company's Business Plan and "Balanced Scorecard".	☐	☐	☐	☐	☐
An employee lead committee carries out the Ministry (Caring) Plan and solicits recommendations and ideas from all employees.	☐	☐	☐	☐	☐
Multiple communication channels are in place to share and celebrate the Ministry (Caring) Plan's activities with all employees and their families.	☐	☐	☐	☐	☐
A percentage of sales or profits are set aside to fund the Ministry (Caring) Plan.	☐	☐	☐	☐	☐
An "I Caught You Caring" program is in place that allows employees to recognize fellow employees who exhibit the Core Value behaviors.	☐	☐	☐	☐	☐

Total your score here: _____

If you scored between 125 and 100 – *Congratulations, you are well on your way.*

If you scored between 75 and 99 – *You have made some great progress with room to grow.*

If you scored under 75 – *Be encouraged, you now have a better idea of the areas to focus and opportunities for improvement.*

No matter what your score, you will find the Companion Handbook a great resource in your life journey to…"Seek What Really Matters" Matthew 6:33

Potential Ministry (Caring) Plan Activities

Provide a corporate chaplain who develops caring relationships with all employees and gives assistance during life issues.
Establish funding for employee crisis needs such as: major medical/dental care, home/car repair, power bills, etc.
Set up a library for adults and children of Christian Books, Bibles, CDs, DVDs.
Create a voluntary prayer and devotion time at work.
Communicate your Mission/Core Values Statement on company: business cards, web site, office plaques, emails, uniforms, t-shirts, product packaging, mouse pads, etc.
Invite local ministries to share with employees their vision/activities and support them financially and with employee volunteer time.
Provide funding to encourage employees to attend or participate in: marriage enrichment retreats, local/overseas short-term mission trips, continuing education, single parenting conferences, personal financial management training, parenting courses, adoption, stop smoking, aging family support groups, medical screenings, substance abuse rehabilitation, etc.
Encourage employee volunteerism by matching volunteer hours with paid time off.
Create an Employee Benevolent Fund that individual employees can contribute to, that is then matched by the company.
Celebrate with gratitude!... employee birthdays, company service anniversaries, wedding anniversaries, promotions, production performance accomplishments, new business, safety achievements, new hires, etc.

Create a "Compassionate Severance Plan" for anyone released by the company which provides outplacement services, resume development assistance and counseling.

Reach out to local needs of your community through employee volunteer projects such as: Habitat For Humanity, Soup Kitchen, Homeless Shelters, Safe Homes, Meals On Wheels, Crisis Pregnancy Centers, Relay For Life, United Way, Neighborhood repair/clean-up days, Student Mentorship, etc.

Sponsor employee family activities: Christmas parties, Easter egg hunts, picnics, sporting events, movie nights, volunteer projects, sports leagues, etc.

Invite pastors to tour your company and show them how their "seed casting" on Sundays has taken root Monday-Saturday.

Join a small group of fellow business leaders for continued training, encouragement and accountability.

Seek new Ministry (Caring) Plan "best practice" thoughts, ideas and activities from other God glorifying companies.

Share Ministry (Caring) Plan thoughts, ideas and activities with other companies seeking to establish their own Ministry (Care) Plan.

We would like to thank Jim Dismore with Kingdom Way Companies (*www.kingdomwayco.org*) and Ron Eads, Business and Workplace Ministry Consultant (*roneads@gmail.com*) for their contribution to the Polydeck Caring Process, the Self Assessment and Potential Activities section of this book.

Corporate
Chaplains

O F A M E R I C A

Our mission is to build caring relationships
with the hope of gaining permission
to share the life changing
Good News of Jesus Christ
in a non-threatening manner.

www.chaplain.org

(800)825-0310 Ext. 777

"Coaching Businesses To Seek What Really Matters"

Our Mission:

To equip and encourage businesses to gradually transform into Christ-centered organizations that:

- Operate on virtue based principles;

- Demonstrate authentic Christian caring, enabling them through the Holy Spirit to lead others to Christ.

We Provide:

† Step by step coaching at no cost

† Customized caring plan (ministry plan) for your business

† Spiritual support and mentoring

† Tools to navigate legal, marketing, human resource and financial barriers

864.205.1265
hiswayatwork@aol.com
www.hiswayatwork.com

For over two decades Dr. Steve O. Steff has served businesses and individuals across the nation as counselor, consultant, and coach. As Founder of Crisis Care International, Steve is recognized as one of the leading experts in crisis response and intervention in the workplace. Steve is seen by his  peers as a pioneer in workplace ministry movement, and has a passion for touching lives for Christ in the workplace. Most recently, Steve is focusing on business coaching and personnel development, providing insight to business leaders and managers in helping them balance their life, while maximizing performance.

Steve holds a doctorate in Leadership and Business Ethics, as well as Masters degrees in both Counseling and Biblical Studies.

Steve and his wife Kathleen are crossing their third decade together, and are the parents of one grown son, Jeremiah.

Companies across the US have benefited from Steve's coaching and consulting. For more information visit *www.TLeadership.com.*